A YOUNG VIC PRODUCTION

T0347847

THE SOLDIERS' FORTUNE

A comedy by Thomas Otway

This production opened at the Young Vic (16 February–31 March 2007)

THE SOLDIERS' FORTUNE

Sir Jolly Jumble **David Bamber**
Lady Dunce **Anne-Marie Duff**
Captain Beaugard **Ray Fearon**
Whore **Kate Feldschreiber**
Sir Davy Dunce **Oliver Ford Davies**
Drawer & Constable **Michael Howcroft**
Vermin **Sam Kenyon**
Sylvia **Kananu Kirimi**
Whore **Lisa Lee Leslie**
Courtine **Alec Newman**
Bloody Bones **James Traherne**
Fourbin **Ben Turner**

Direction **David Lan**
Set **Lizzie Clachan**
Costumes **Joan Wadge**
Lighting **Rick Fisher**
Composer **Tim Sutton**
Choreography **Alexandra Reynolds**
Sound **Paul Groothuis**
Casting **Julia Horan**
Costume Supervision **Lisa Aitken**
Assistant Director **Vik Sivalingam**
Stage Manager **Sophie Gabszewicz**
Deputy Stage Manager **Vicky Gibson**
Assistant Stage Manager **Claire Jowett**

BIOGRAPHIES

David Bamber Sir Jolly Jumble

Theatre includes: *Otherwise Engaged* (Criterion); *Lisbon Traviata* (King's Head); *The Glee Club* (Bush/Duchess Theatre); *Troilus and Cressida, The Merchant of Venice, Racing Demon, The Wind in the Willows* (National Theatre); *The Arbor, Three Birds Alighting on a Field, My Night with Reg* (Winner of Olivier Award 1995 for Best Actor; Royal Court). Television includes: *Rome* (HBO/BBC); *Pride and Prejudice, Daniel Deronda* (BBC); *Trial & Retribution* (ITV). Film includes: *Miss Potter* (dir. Chris Noonan); *High Hopes* (dir. Mike Leigh).

Anne-Marie Duff Lady Dunce

Theatre includes: *The Daughter in Law* (Young Vic); *Days of Wine and Roses* (Donmar Warehouse); *King Lear, War and Peace* (National Theatre); *Collected Stories* (Nominated for Olivier Award 2000 for Best Supporting Actress; West End); *Vassa* (Almeida Theatre). Television includes: *Elizabeth – The Virgin Queen*; *Shameless* (Nominated for BAFTA 2005 and 2006 for Best Actress); *The History of Mr Polly*; *Charles II*. Film includes: *Notes on a Scandal; Born Equal; Garage; Magdalene Sisters; Enigma*.

Ray Fearon Captain Beaugard

Theatre includes: *Sing Yer Heart Out for the Lads* (National Theatre); *World Music* (Donmar Warehouse); *Pericles, Othello, Don Carlos, Romeo & Juliet, The White Devil* (RSC); *Venice Preserved* (Almeida Theatre). Film includes: *Harry Potter and the Philosopher's Stone* (Warner Bros.);

Clandestine Marriage (Portman Films); *Hamlet* (Fishmonger Films). Television includes: *Coronation Street, Prime Suspect, Band of Gold* (Granada); *Revelations* (NBC); *Keen Eddie* (Paramount British Pictures); *Waking the Dead 4* (BBC).

Kate Feldschreiber Whore

Theatre includes: *Chess, Little Shop of Horrors, Grease* (Imperial College London); *Anything Goes, Kiss Me, Kate, Pirates of Penzance, The Biograph Girl, Something's Afoot* (Budleigh Salterton); *Elegies for Angels, Punks And Raging Queens, A Funny Thing Happened On The Way To The Forum* (London Oratory). Credits with GSA Conservatoire include: *Lucky Stiff, Galileo, Sweeney Todd, Oklahoma!*.

Oliver Ford Davies Sir Davy Dunce

Theatre includes: *The Life of Galileo, Playing with Fire, Racing Demon* (Winner of 1990 Olivier Award for Best Actor), *David Hare Trilogy* (National Theatre); *Larkin with Women, The Linden Tree, King Cromwell* (Orange Tree); *Darwin in Malibu* (Hampstead); *Absolutely! (Perhaps)* (Wyndham's Theatre). Film includes: *Atonement* (Tallis Pictures); *Star Wars: I, II & III* (Jak Productions); *The Mother* (Mother Productions); *Johnny English* (Rogue Male Films). Television includes: *David Copperfield* (BBC); *Kavanagh QC – 5 series* (Carlton); *The Way We Live Now* (Deep Indigo Productions).

Michael Howcroft
Drawer & Constable

Theatre includes: *Amadeus* (Wiltons Music Hall); *As You Like It* (Young Vic/Wyndhams Theatre); *Sweeney Todd* (Trafalgar Studios, Watermill Theatre & tour); *Carmen, Cinderella, Fiddler on the Roof, Piaf* (Watermill, Newbury); *Privates on Parade* (New Victoria, Stoke); *Poor Ted* (OnO Theatre). As Musical Director: *Cinderella* (Broxbourne); *Millennium Dance 2006* (Embassy Theatre); *Sweeney Todd* (No.1 Tour 2006); *Annie* (Aberystwyth); *Cinderella* (Porthcawl).

Sam Kenyon Vermin

Theatre includes: *Amadeus* (Wiltons Music Hall); *The Mushroom Pickers* (Southwark Playhouse); *Burial at Thebes* (Nottingham Playhouse); *As You Like It* (Young Vic/Wyndhams Theatre); *Sweeney Todd* (Nominated for Olivier Award 2005; UK Tour and West End); *Jerry Springer – The Opera* (BAC/Edinburgh); *Ion, Les Justes* (Gate Theatre); *Stairs to the Roof* (Minerva Theatre); *Weill & Lenya* (New End Theatre); *Rough Crossing* (Upstairs at the Gatehouse); *Macbeth, Othello Music, Love* (BAC); *Tropical Tree* (Lyric Studio); *Demon Headmaster* (UK Tour); *A-Ronne, Con Voce* (Almeida Opera). Film includes: *Venus* (dir. Roger Michell).

Kananu Kirimi Sylvia

Theatre includes: *Romeo & Juliet, The Tempest* (The Globe); *Paradise Lost* (Bristol Old Vic); *A Doll's House* (Southwark Playhouse); *Fathers and Eggs* (Company of Angels/Quicksilver); *The Tempest, Pericles* (RSC); *Les Liasons Dangereuses* (Liverpool Everyman and Playhouse); *A Raisin in the Sun* (Young Vic). Film includes: *The Queen* (dir. Stephen Frears); *Trauma* (dir. Marc Evans); *Small Love* (dir. Manu Kurewa). Television includes: *Sea of Souls* (Carnival Films); *Waking the Dead* (BBC); *The Royal* (ITV). Radio includes: *McLevy* (BBC Radio 4).

Lisa Lee Leslie Whore

Theatre includes: *Hansel & Gretel* (Theatre Royal, Northampton); *As You Like It* (Young Vic/Wyndhams Theatre); *Mirandolina* (Manchester Royal Exchange); *Romeo & Juliet* (RSC). Television includes: *The Big Breakfast* (Channel 4).

Alec Newman Courtine

Theatre includes: *Andorra* (Young Vic); *The Recruiting Officer* (Chichester Festival Theatre); *Plenty* (Albery Theatre); *Certain Young Men* (Almeida Theatre); *The Glass Menagerie, Translations* (Royal Lyceum, Edinburgh). Film includes: *The Fifth Patient* (dir. Amir Mann); *Constellation* (dir. Jordan Walker Pearlmain); *Four Corners of Suburbia* (dir. Elizabeth Puccini); *The Principles Of Lust* (dir. Penny Woolcock); *Bright Young Things* (dir. Stephen Fry). Television includes: *The Acid Test, Spooks, Cortes* (BBC); *Frankenstein* (Hallmark); *Dune* (Sci Fi Channel); *Angel* (WB); *Tru Calling* (FOX).

James Traherne Bloody Bones

Theatre includes: *Rapunzel* (BAC & Kneehigh Theatre); *The Thieves Carnival* (Watermill Theatre); *Tristan & Yseult* (Kneehigh & Australia, New Zealand tour); *Junk* (Bristol Old Vic); *Johnny Blue* (Oxford Stage Company); *Caledonian Road* (Almeida Theatre); *Twelfth Night, The Hired Man* (Theatre by the Lake); *Holes* (Stratford East); *Presto, or The Secret Life of Swift and Gulliver* (Group K/Riverside Studios). **Television includes:** *Supergrass; The Bill; Go Now; Jenner; Dream Team.*

Ben Turner Fourbin

Theatre includes: *As You Like It* (Young Vic/Wyndhams Theatre); *Outlying Islands* (Theatre Royal, Bath); *Measure For Measure, Habeus Corpus* (Sir Peter Hall tour); *Charley's Aunt* (Northcott Theatre); *The Arab Israeli Cook Book* (Gate Theatre); *A Midsummer Night's Dream* (Sheffield Crucible); *Caligula* (Donmar Warehouse); *Cahoot's Macbeth* (King's Head); *The Merchant Of Venice* (RSC). **Film includes:** *Syriana* (dir. Steven Gagan); *Bilingual* (dir. Chamoun Issa). **Television includes:** *Dr Who, Love Soup* (BBC), *Alive* (Channel 4); *As If* (Carnival Films).

David Lan Direction

David Lan is artistic director of the Young Vic where he has directed *'Tis Pity She's a Whore, Julius Caesar, A Raisin in the Sun* (2001 and 2005), *Doctor Faustus, The Daughter in Law* and *The Skin of Our Teeth.* Other productions include: *Pericles* (NT Studio) *The Glass Menagerie* (Watford) and *As You Like It* (Wyndhams as part of the 2004/6 Walkabout).

For the BBC Omnibus series he produced and directed *Artist Unknown* (1995) and *Royal Court Diaries* (1996).

His many plays, screenplays, adaptations and opera libretti have been produced by the Royal Court, the Almeida, the National Theatre, the RSC, BBC TV and Radio, Channel Four and the Young Vic.

He was writer in residence at the Royal Court 1995/7. He has also published an anthropological study *Guns and Rain: Guerrillas and Spirit Mediums in Zimbabwe.*

Since joining the Young Vic in 2000, he has established the Genesis Directors Project, the Jerwood Young Directors Award and the Young Vic Award and has led the just completed rebuild of the theatre. In 2004 the Young Vic received an Olivier Award for 'an audacious season under the artistic leadership of David Lan'.

Lizzie Clachan Set

Lizzie was a founder member of Shunt in 1998 and since then has worked with the company to devise and design all productions, including: *Amato Saltone, Tropicana, Dance Bear Dance, The Tennis Show* and *The Ballad of Bobby Francois.* For The Royal Court: *On Insomnia and Midnight, Woman & Scarecrow* and *Ladybird.* For the RSC: *Days of Significance* and *The American Pilot.* For National Theatre of Scotland: *Miss Julie* and *Gobbo.* Also: *Bedtime Story* and *The End of the Beginning* (Young Vic); *Factory Girls* (Arcola); *Ether Frolics* (Shunt /Sound & Fury); *All in the Timing* (Peepolykus national tour); *Moonstone* (The Royal Exchange, Manchester).

Joan Wadge Costumes

Theatre includes: *Drunk Enough to Say I Love You; Hergé's Adventures of Tintin; Festen; A Number; Plasticine; Afore Night Come* and *Albert Speer.* **Television includes:** *Under the Greenwood Tree* (dir. Nick Laughland, prod. Jeremy Gwilt for Ecosse Production Company); *Heaven on Earth* (dir. Stuart Orme for ITV); *Ivanhoe* (dir. Stuart Orme, prod. Jeremy Gwilt for BBC); *Henry IV parts 1 & 2* (dir. John Caird for BBC); *Adventures of the Worst Witch Series 1 & 2* (prod. Angela Beeching for ITV); *House of Elliot* – 1st and 3rd series (prod. Jeremy Gwilt for BBC). Until 1996 Joan was a member of the BBC design department during which time she was nominated for Bafta and Emmy awards.

Rick Fisher Lighting

Originally from Philadelphia, Rick has been working in British theatre for over twenty years. He is currently Chairman of the British Association of Lighting Designers.

Credits for Young Vic: *Hergé's Adventures of Tintin*, *Afore Night Come*, *Red Demon* and *Peribanez*.

Recent theatre work includes: *Billy Elliot, the Musical* (Victoria Palace), *Sugar Babies, On Insomnia* and *Midnight* (Royal Court). Recent opera includes: *Betrothal in a Monastery* (Glyndebourne); *The Little Prince* (New York City Opera, Houston Grand Opera); *Peter Grimes* (Santa Fe). Dance includes: *Swan Lake* (London / Los Angeles / Broadway) for Matthew Bourne's Adventures in Motion Pictures.

Awards include: Bronze Medal for Lighting Design at the 2005 World Stage Design show in Toronto. 1998, 1994 Olivier Award Winner for Best Lighting Design; and a Tony Award for *An Inspector Calls* (Broadway).

Tim Sutton Composer

Tim Sutton is the Musical Director of Music Theatre 4 Youth and Guest Conductor of Voce Chamber Choir. He recently conducted a new production of *Sweeney Todd* at Värmlands Opera, Sweden. Tim's choral work is published by Novello Ltd.

Recent work includes music for the film *I Said So Little, Thought Latching Onto Thought* (Place Prize 2007); *Women Beware Women* (RSC); *As You Desire Me* for which he was also vocal coach to Kristin Scott Thomas (Playhouse); *Knight of the Burning Pestle* (Young Vic/Barbican); and *As You Like It* (Wyndham's). Tim has also provided music for three *Doctor Who* audio plays (Big Finish), to be broadcast on BBC7 this year. Original musicals include *Tilting at Windmills, Such Sweet Thunder* and *Oak*.

Musical direction includes: *Marat/Sade* (National Theatre); *Trouble in Tahiti* (BAC); *Hymn to Love* (Mercury Colchester, Drill Hall, Traverse Edinburgh and BBC Radio 3); *China Song* (Plymouth Drum and touring); *Marie* (Basingstoke, Keswick and touring); *The Mikado* (Newcastle-under-Lyme, Orange Tree Richmond); *The Mother* (Keswick); and *The Wind in the Willows* (Birmingham Rep). Work as Chorus Master includes *The Little Prince* (BBC2) and *Showboat* at the Royal Albert Hall.

Alexandra Reynolds Choreography

In her career as both performer and choreographer, Alex has collaborated with some of Europe's most exciting and innovative directors. Over the last 10 years her distinctive choreography has featured in commercials, music videos, opera, theatre, fashion and live spectacle. She was nominee for the Craft Award at the Women in Film and Television Awards 2002. Most recently she choreographed the hugely successful Supernature world tour for Goldfrapp.

Paul Groothuis Sound

Paul was born in the Netherlands and came to the UK in 1979 to train as a stage manager at Central School of Speech and Drama. Having spent 3 years working as a Recording Engineer in a London Studio, he joined the Sound Department of the National Theatre in 1984 and stayed until 2003. As a member of the RNT's Sound Department he designed the sound for over 120 productions. His current projects include *The Lightning Play* at the Almeida Theatre, *Merry Wives – The Musical* at the RSC, *Porgy and Bess* with Trevor Nunn at the Savoy Theatre, and in 2007, *Man of Mode* with Nicholas Hytner and *Rose Tattoo* with Steven Pimlott, both at the NT. Paul is Associate to the RNT Sound Department and Sound Consultant for Sir Peter Hall's Rose of Kingston Theatre project. In 2006 and again in 2007 Paul will spend time as Guest Lecturer at the Hong Kong Academy of Performing Arts.

Julia Horan Casting

Recent theatre credits include: *Dying for It* (Almeida Theatre); *Bad Jazz, A Brief History of Helen of Troy* (ATC); *Pool (No Water)* (Frantic Assembly/Lyric Hammersmith); *Gaddafi – A Living Myth* (ENO/ Asian Dub Foundation); *Hergé's Adventures of Tintin* (Young Vic/ bite:-05, Barbican); *The Prayer Room* (Birmingham Rep/EIF); *As You Like It* (Wyndham's Theatre); *One Under* (Tricycle Theatre); *Anna in the Tropics, Yellowman* (Hampstead Theatre); *Othello* (Cheek by Jowl), *The Skin of Our Teeth, Hobson's Choice, The Daughter-In-Law, Homebody Kabul, A Raisin in the Sun, Six Characters Looking for an Author* (Young Vic);

The Morris, Port Authority, Urban Legend, The Kindness of Strangers (Liverpool Everyman); *The Girl on the Sofa* (EIF/Schaubühne Theatre, Berlin); *Original Sin* (Crucible, Sheffield); *Antarctica* (Savoy); *The Weir* (Duke of York's); *The Force of Change, Made of Stone, Local, Trade, About a Boy, Yard Gal, Holy Mothers, Last Dance at Dum-Dum* (Royal Court).

Assistant Director

Vik Sivalingam

Credits as director: *Please Find Attached* (King's Head); *Dreaming* (Brighton College); *The Waiting Line* (Birmingham Arts Fest); *The Hard Way* (Soho Theatre Studio); *Human Rights* (Sir John Mills Theatre, Ipswich); *Blue/Orange* (New Wolsey Theatre Studio); *Girlfriends* (co-directed with Pete Rowe, BAC); *Day Trippers* (New Wolsey Theatre, Ipswich & Theatr Clwyd); *Swingin' In Mid-Dream!* (Albany, London).

Credits as assistant director: *The Price, Private Lives, The Tempest, Sugar* (New Wolsey Theatre); *Troilus & Cressida* (directed by Jonathan Munby).

Vik holds an MFA in Theatre Directing from Birkbeck, University of London.

THE YOUNG VIC

We are this country's leading home for younger theatre artists, especially directors. By presenting seasons of work by new directors in tandem with some of the great directors of the world – mingling youth and experience, ambition and genius – we hope to make the Young Vic one of the most exciting theatres in the world.

Many people, especially the young, believe that theatre belongs to 'others' of another class or another generation. But artists create for everyone. So we keep our prices low and, through an extensive program of Teaching, Participation and Research, we make a priority of finding and creating new audiences. 10% of our tickets are given away each year, irrespective of box-office pressure.

We believe a theatre should be a place of energy, intelligence and pleasure.

Join us in our new theatre whenever you can.

Young Vic
66 The Cut
London SE1 8LZ

www.youngvic.org
Tickets & information 020 7922 2922
Administration 020 7922 2800

The Young Vic is a company limited by guarantee, registered in England No. 1188209.
VAT registration No. 236 673 348
The Young Vic (registered charity number 268876) receives public funding from

THE NAKED PLAYWRIGHT
AN INTRODUCTION BY DAVID LAN

THE TEXT GIVEN HERE differs from the complete text of the play by, perhaps, five per cent. The only change is in shortening. A dozen words which have so lost their currency as to be incomprehensible have been replaced by more recently coined equivalents. I have broken up the scenes of Act Four in a different way and re-arranged about twenty lines. Apart from this, the play is entirely Otway's.

The point is worth making because Otway's sensibility, especially as concerns sexual matters, is remarkably modern – so modern, in fact, that the shock of finding the deeply contradictory nature of sexual experience presented in quite so undisguised a way might lead an audience at our 2007 production to the view that the text has been tampered with, 'brought up to date'. Not at all.

And this, I believe, is one of the reasons – there are others – that *The Soldiers' Fortune* earns its occasional but regular revivals. (It struts the London stage about once every twenty years.) I love it because, the deeper you dig into it, the more you feel that the play simply flowed out of Otway, with all its absurd, angular, imperfect vivacity, whether he wished it to or not.

Of course, it leans heavily on the taken-for-granted conventions of the theatre of his time. You can feel Moliere's *The School for Wives* discretely in the background. The theme of 'soldiers from the wars returning' is as old as the theatre itself.

And yet, I think, there is something uniquely brazen about this play, uniquely 'in-yer-face', to use the current cliché. We know from the scant biography of Otway available that he served the French in the disastrous wars in Holland and returned to England as penniless as are Beaugard and Courtine in Act One, Scene One. We know from his letters that he was as profoundly in love with a woman –probably Mrs Barry, an actress – who left him for another ('I love you, I dote on you; desire makes me mad when I am near you, and despair when I am from you'), as, perhaps, Beaugard is with Lady Dunce.

All the world of the play lies in that 'perhaps'. What does Beaugard *really* feel about Lady Dunce? It's hard to say. Running right through the play is an ambivalence about the value of deep emotion that catches at the heart because the characters seem so unaware of what they are doing and why. They're driven by lust – the business of farce. But their lust seems fuelled by anger, by hurt, by humiliation, by distress – the business of tragedy.

In fact, to say 'tragedy' is to go much too far – except perhaps for the fate of Lady Dunce, abandoned at the play's end to a life of, I would guess, unsustainable compromise. The play advertises itself in its first edition of 1681 as 'a comedy' and if we aren't true to this in our production we fail our author. But it's a comedy that feeds not on embarrassment, like 19th- and 20th-century farce, but on trauma – and on its concomitants: bewilderment and rage.

All of which makes it feel like it was written last week.

In his brief day (1651–1685) Thomas Otway was most famous for his two full-blown tragedies, the fairly frequently revived *Venice Preserved* and the forgotten *The Orphan*, both written in a verse that was praised as the equal of Shakespeare's. *The Soldiers' Fortune*, written in prose, was his most successful comedy.

Unlike many later and better-known comic playwrights of the Restoration, Otway, in this play at least, allowed himself to be seen naked on the stage. It's my guess that he relished the experience. I hope you do too.

David Lan, 2007

Thomas Otway

THE SOLDIERS' FORTUNE

Edited by David Lan

OBERON BOOKS
LONDON

Characters

CAPTAIN BEAUGARD

COURTINE

LADY DUNCE

SIR DAVY DUNCE

SIR JOLLY JUMBLE

SYLVIA

FOURBIN

BLOODY BONES

VERMIN

FRISK

DRAWER

WHORES

A CONSTABLE

WATCHMEN

Scene: London 1680

ACT ONE

SCENE ONE

The Mall.

Enter BEAUGARD, COURTINE and FOURBIN.

BEAUGARD: A pox o' fortune! Thou art always teasing me about fortune. Thou risest of a morning with ill luck in thy mouth, nay, never eat'st a dinner but thou sigh'st two hours after with worrying where to get the next. Fortune be damned since the world's so wide.

COURTINE: As wide as it is, 'tis so thronged and crammed with knaves and fools an honest man can hardly get a living in it.

BEAUGARD: Do rail, Courtine, do. It may get thee employment.

COURTINE: At you I ought to rail. 'Twas your fault we left our employment abroad to come home and be loyal and now we as loyally starve.

BEAUGARD: Did not thy ancestors do it before thee, man? I tell thee, loyalty and starving are one.

COURTINE: 'Tis a fine equipage I am reduced to. This flopping hat pinned up on one side with a sandy, weather-beaten peruke, dirty linen and, to complete the figure, a long, scandalous iron sword jarring at my heels like a –

BEAUGARD: Snarling thou mean'st, like its master.

COURTINE: My companions, villains that undervalue damnation, will forswear themselves for a dinner and hang their fathers for half a crown.

BEAUGARD: I am ashamed to hear a soldier talk of starving.

COURTINE: Why, what shall I do? I can't steal!

BEAUGARD: No, thou canst not steal, Ned, but thou hast other vices enough for any industrious young fellow to live comfortably upon.

COURTINE: What, wouldst thou have me turn rascal and run cheating up and down the town? I would no more keep a blockhead company and endure his nauseous nonsense in hopes to con him than I would, for a pension, be a drudge to an old woman with rheumatic eyes, hollow teeth and stinking breath.

BEAUGARD: How well this niceness becomes thee! Surely an old lady's pension need not be so despicable in the eyes of a disbanded officer as times go, Ned.

COURTINE: I am glad, Beaugard, you think so.

BEAUGARD: Why, thou shalt think so too. Be ruled by me and I'll bring thee into good company. Families, Courtine, and such families where formality's a scandal and pleasure's the only business, where the women are all wanton and witty, you rogue.

COURTINE: What, some of your Wapping acquaintance that you made last time you came over here to England for recruits and spirited away your landlady's daughter with you into France?

BEAUGARD: I'll bring thee, Courtine, where lewdness is laudable, where thou shalt wallow in pleasure, revel all day and every night lie in the arms of melting beauty, sweet as roses and as springs refreshing.

COURTINE: Prithee don't talk thus. A pox on whores when a man has not money to make 'em comfortable.

BEAUGARD: That shall shower upon us in abundance. Know to thy everlasting amazement, all this dropped out of the clouds today.

COURTINE: Ha! Gold, by this light!

FOURBIN: Out of the clouds!

BEAUGARD: (*To FOURBIN.*) Ay, gold! Does it not smell of the sweet hand that sent it? Smell, you dog!

FOURBIN smells the handful of gold and gathers up some pieces in his mouth.

FOURBIN: Truly, sir, of heavenly sweetness and very refreshing.

COURTINE: Dear Beaugard, if thou hast any good nature in thee, if thou wouldst not have me hang myself before my time, tell me where the devil haunts that helped thee to this that I may go make a bargain with him. Speak or I am a lost man.

BEAUGARD: Why this devil, to which I have given my soul already and must, I suppose, give my body very speedily, lives I know not where and may for aught I know be a real devil. But if he be, 'tis the best-natured devil in Beelzebub's dominion.

COURTINE: But how came the gold then?

BEAUGARD: I lately happened into the acquaintance of a very reverend pimp, a good natured, public-spirited fellow that is never so happy as when he is bringing good people together and promoting understanding betwixt the sexes. Nay, rather than want employment, he will go from one end of the town to t'other to procure my lord's little dog to be civil to my lady's little bitch.

COURTINE: A worthy member of the commonwealth!

BEAUGARD: This noble person – but Fourbin can give you a more particular account. (*To FOURBIN.*) Sweet sir, if you please, tell us the story of the first encounter betwixt you and Sir Jolly Jumble.

FOURBIN: Sir, it shall be done. Walking one day upon the Piazza I chance to encounter a person of worthy appearance, his beard and hair white, his countenance ruddy, plump, smooth and cheerful who, perceiving me with air which might well inform him I was a person of no inconsiderable quality, came respectfully up to me and humbly inquired, 'What is it o'clock?' I, understanding by the question that he was a man of business, told him it was but nicely turned of three.

BEAUGARD: Very court-like, civil, quaint and new.

FOURBIN: After some questions *pour passer le temps*, he was pleased to offer me the courtesy of a glass of wine. I told him I very seldom drink but, if he so pleased, I would do myself the honour to present him with a dish of meat at an eating-house hard by.

COURTINE: This squire of thine, Beaugard, is as accomplished as any I ever saw.

BEAUGARD: Let the rogue go on.

FOURBIN: In short, as soon as we entered the room, 'I am your most humble servant, sir,' says he. 'I am the meanest of your vassals, sir,' said I. 'I am very happy in lighting into the acquaintance of so worthy a gentleman,' said he. 'Worthy Sir Jolly' – for by that time I had groped out his title – 'I kiss your hands from the bottom of my heart which I am ready to lay at your feet.'

COURTINE: Well and what replied the knight?

FOURBIN: Nothing. His sense was transported with admiration of my parts. I told him those that know me well call me the Chevalier Fourbin, a cadet of the ancient family of the Fourbinois and that I have had the honour to serve the great monarch of France in his wars against the Dutch where I contracted intimacy with a gallant English officer in his service, one Captain Beaugard.

BEAUGARD: O, sir, you did me too much honour. What a true-bred rogue's this!

COURTINE: But the money, Fourbin, the money.

FOURBIN: 'Beaugard, hum,' says he. 'A black man, is he not?' 'Ay,' says I, 'blackish.' 'Dark brown, full-faced?' 'Yes.' 'A sly, subtle, observing eye?' 'The same.' 'A strong-built, well-made man?' 'Right.' 'A devilish fellow for a wench, I warrant him! Beaugard! A thundering fellow for a wench! I must be acquainted with him.'

COURTINE: But to the money. That's the thing I would be acquainted with.

BEAUGARD: This civil gentleman comes yesterday morning to my lodging and, seeing my picture in miniature, told me with the greatest ecstasy in the world that that was the thing he came about. He said a lady of his acquaintance had some favourable thoughts of me. 'Egad,' says he, 'she's a hummer, ah-h-h!' So without more ado he begs me to lend him my picture till dinner. Away he scuttled with as great joy as if he had found the philosopher's stone. At dinner, after a thousand grimaces to show how much he was pleased, instead of my picture he presents me with the contents and tells me the lady desires me to accept 'em as payment for the picture which she was as much transported by as by the original.

COURTINE: Ha!

BEAUGARD: Whereabout this quality lies in me, Ned, the devil take me if I know – but the fates, Ned, the fates!

COURTINE: A curse on the fates! Of all strumpets fortune's the basest. 'Twas fortune made me a soldier, a rogue in red, the grievance of the nation. Fortune made the peace just when we were upon the brink of war. Then fortune disbanded us and lost us two months' pay. Fortune gave us debentures instead of ready money and by very good fortune I sold mine and lost heartily by it. I hope the grinding, ill-natured dog that bought it will never get a shilling for't.

BEAUGARD: Leave off thy railing, for shame. He looks like a cur that barks for want of bones. Come, times may mend and an honest soldier be in fashion again.

COURTINE: Those greasy, fat, unwieldy, wheezing rogues that live at home and brood over their money bags. When a fit of fear of the French is upon 'em, if one of us pass by, all the family's at the door to cry, 'Heaven bless you!' But when the fear is over, every bawd roars out, 'Out, ye lousy redcoat rakehells! Out, ye locusts of the nation! You are the dogs that would plunder our shops and ravish our daughters.'

BEAUGARD: Fourbin!

FOURBIN: Your worship's pleasure?

BEAUGARD: Run like the rogue you are, find Sir Jolly and desire him to meet me at the Blue Posts in the Haymarket about twelve. We'll dine together.

Exit FOURBIN.

In the meantime, Ned, here's half the prize. We have shared good fortune and bad shall never part us.

COURTINE: Well, thou wilt certainly die in a ditch. Hast thou no more grace than to part with thy money to thy friend? I grant you, a gentleman may lie for his friend, pimp for his friend, hang for his friend but to part with ready money is the devil.

BEAUGARD: Stand aside. Either I am mistaken or yonder's Sir Jolly. Now, Courtine, will I show thee the flower of knighthood.

Enter SIR JOLLY JUMBLE.

Ah, Sir Jolly!

SIR JOLLY: My hero! My darling! My Ganymede! How dost thou? Strong! Wanton! Lusty! Rampant! Ha, ah, ah! She's thine, boy, od, she's thine. Plump, soft, smooth, wanton! Ha, ah, ah! Ah rogue, ah rogue! Here's shoulders, here's shape! There's a foot and leg! Here's a leg, here's a leg! Qua-a-a-a-a!

He squeaks like a cat and tickles BEAUGARD's legs.

COURTINE: What an old goat's this?

SIR JOLLY: Child, child, child, who's that? A friend o' thine? A pretty fellow, od, a very pretty fellow and a strong dog, I'll warrant him. How dost do, dear heart? Prithee, let me kiss thee. I'll swear and vow I will kiss thee. Ha, ha, he, he, he, he! A toad, a toad, ah toa-a-a-ad!

COURTINE: Sir, I am your humble servant.

BEAUGARD: But the lady, Sir Jolly, the lady? How does the lady? What says the lady, Sir Jolly?

SIR JOLLY: What says the lady? Why, she says – she says – od, she has a delicate lip, such a lip, so red, so hard, so plump, so blub. I fancy I am eating cherries every time I think of't – and for her neck and breasts and her – od's life! I'll say no more, not a word more. But I know, I know –

BEAUGARD: I am sorry for that with all my heart. Do you know her, say you, and would you put off your used goods, your offal upon me?

SIR JOLLY: Hush, hush, hush! Have a care. As I live and breathe, not I. Alack and well-a-day, I am a poor old fellow, decayed and done. All's gone with me, gentlemen, but my good nature. Od, I love to know how matters go, though – now and then to see a pretty wench and a young fellow touse and rouse and frowze and mouse. Od, I love a young fellow dearly, faith, dearly!

COURTINE: This is the most extraordinary rogue I ever met.

BEAUGARD: But, Sir Jolly, in the first place, you must know I have sworn never to marry.

SIR JOLLY: I would not have thee, man. I am a bachelor myself and have been a whoremaster all my life. Besides, she's married already, man. Her husband's an old, greasy, untoward, ill-natured, slovenly, tobacco-taking cuckold – but plaguy jealous.

BEAUGARD: Already a cuckold, Sir Jolly?

SIR JOLLY: No – that shall be, my boy. Thou shalt make him one and I'll pimp for thee, dear heart. And shan't I hold the door? Shan't I peep, ha? Shan't I, you devil? You little dog, shan't I?

BEAUGARD: What is it I'd not grant my patron?

SIR JOLLY: And then – dost hear? – I have a lodging for thee in my own house. Dost hear, old soul? She lives the very next door, man. There's but a wall to part her chamber and thine. And then for a peep-hole, od's fish, I have a peep-hole for thee. 'Sbud, I'll show thee, I'll show thee.

BEAUGARD: But when, Sir Jolly? I am in haste.

SIR JOLLY: Why, this very night, man. Poor rogue's in haste. But, hear you, shan't we dine together?

BEAUGARD: With all my heart.

SIR JOLLY: Get you before and bespeak dinner at the Blue Posts while I stay behind and gather up a dish of whores for a dessert.

COURTINE: Be sure that they be lewd, drunken, stripping whores, Sir Jolly, that won't be affectedly squeamish and troublesome.

SIR JOLLY: I warrant you.

COURTINE: I love a well-disciplined whore that shows all the tricks of her profession with a wink, like an old soldier that understands all his exercise by beat of drum.

SIR JOLLY: Ah thief, sayest thou so! I must be better acquainted with that fellow. He has a notable nose.

BEAUGARD: Well, Sir Jolly, you'll not fail us?

SIR JOLLY: Fail ye? Am I a knight? Hark ye, boys, I'll muster this evening such a regiment of rampant, roaring, roisterous whores that shall make more noise than if all the cats in the Haymarket were in conjunction – whores, ye rogues, that shall swear with you, drink with you, talk bawdy with you, fight with you, scratch with you, lie with you and go to the devil with you. Shan't we be very merry, ha?

COURTINE: As merry as wine, women and wickedness can make us.

SIR JOLLY: Od, that's well said again. I love a fellow that is very wicked. Methinks there's a spirit in him. There's a sort of a tantara-rara, tantara-rara, ah, ah-h-h! Well, and won't ye, when the women come, won't ye? And shall I not see a little sport amongst you? Well, get ye gone. Ah rogues, ah rogues! Da, da. I'll be with you. Da, da.

Exeunt BEAUGARD and COURTINE.

Enter several WHORES.

FIRST WHORE: Well, I'll swear, madam, 'tis the finest evening. I love the Mall mightily.

SECOND WHORE: Really, and so do I because there's always good company and one meets with such civilities from everybody.

THIRD WHORE: Ay, and then I love extremely to show myself here when I am very fine to vex those poor devils that call themselves virtues and are scandalous. O crimine, who's yonder! Sir Jolly Jumble, I vow.

FIRST WHORE: O Papa, Papa! Where have you been these two days, Papa?

SECOND WHORE: You are a precious father to take no more care of your children. We might be dead, you naughty Daddy, you.

SIR JOLLY: Dead, my poor fubs! Od, I had rather all the relations I have were dead, adad I had. Get you gone, you little devils. Bubbies! O law, there's bubbies! Od, I'll bite 'em, od, I will.

FIRST WHORE: Nay, fie, Papa! I swear you'll make me angry unless you carry us and treat us tonight. You have promised me a treat this week. Won't you, Papa?

SECOND WHORE: Ay, won't you, Dad?

SIR JOLLY: Od's so, od's so, well remembered! Get you gone, don't stay talking, get you gone. Yonder's a great lord, the Lord Beaugard, and his cousin the baron, the count, the marquis, the Lord knows what, Monsieur Courtine, newly come to town, od's so.

THIRD WHORE: O law, where, Daddy, where? O dear, a lord!

FIRST WHORE: Well, you are the purest Papa. But where be dey mun, Papa?

SIR JOLLY: I won't tell you, you gypsies, so I won't – except you tickle me. 'Sbud, they are brave fellows all, tall, and not a bit small. Od, one of 'em has a devilish deal of money.

FIRST WHORE: O dear, but which is he, Papa?

SECOND WHORE: Shan't I be in love with him, Daddy?

SIR JOLLY: What, nobody tickle me? Tickle me a little, Mally. Tickle me a little, Jenny. Do!

They tickle him.

He, he, he, he, he, he! No more! Oh dear, oh dear! Poor rogues! So, so, no more! Nay, if you do, if you do, od, I'll, I'll, I'll –

THIRD WHORE: What will you do?

SIR JOLLY: Come along with me. Sneak after me at a distance that nobody take notice. Swingeing fellows, Mally, swingeing fellows, Jenny! A devilish deal of money! Get you afore me then, you little didappers, ye wasps, ye wagtails! Get you gone, I say! Swingeing fellows!

SCENE TWO

A room in SIR DAVY's house

Enter LADY DUNCE and SYLVIA.

LADY DUNCE: Die a maid, Sylvia? What a scandalous resolution's that? Five thousand pounds to your portion and leave it all to hospitals? Fie for shame!

SYLVIA: Indeed, such another charming animal as your consort, Sir David, might do much for me. 'Tis a blessing to lie all night by a horse-load of diseases – a beastly, unsavoury, old, groaning, grunting, wheezing wretch that smells of the grave he's going to. From such a hair-cloth next my skin, heaven deliver me!

LADY DUNCE: Thou mistakest the use of a husband, Sylvia. They are not meant for bedfellows. Heretofore, indeed, 'twas a fulsome fashion to lie o' nights with a husband – but the world's improved and customs altered.

SYLVIA: Pray instruct me then what the use of a husband is.

LADY DUNCE: To be in waiting instead of an usher for ceremony's sake on set days and particular occasions. But the friend, cousin, is the jewel invaluable.

SYLVIA: But Sir David, madam, if I am not mistaken, has a nature too jealous to be blinded.

LADY DUNCE: So much the better. The jealous fool is easiest of all to deceive. For observe, there's never jealousy without there's fondness which, if a woman make right use of, a husband's fears shall not so wake him as his doting on her shall blind him.

SYLVIA: Is your piece of mortality such a doting doodle? Is he so very fond of you?

LADY DUNCE: No – but he has the vanity to think that I am very fond of him. And if he be jealous, 'tis not so much for fear that I abuse him as fear that in time I may. Therefore he imposes this confinement on me – though he has other divertisements that take him off from my enjoyment, which make him so loathsome no woman but must hate him.

SYLVIA: His private divertisements I am a stranger to.

LADY DUNCE: His person is incomparably odious. He has such a breath one kiss of him were enough to cure the fits of the mother. 'Tis worse than asafoetida.

SYLVIA: O hideous!

LADY DUNCE: Everything that's nasty he affects. Clean linen, he says, is unwholesome and, to make him more charming, he's continually eating garlic and chewing tobacco.

SYLVIA: Faugh! This is love! This is the blessing of matrimony!

LADY DUNCE: Rail not so unreasonably against love, Sylvia. As I have dealt freely and acknowledged to thee the passion I have for Beaugard, so methinks Sylvia need not conceal her good thoughts of her friend. Do not I know Courtine sticks in your stomach?

SYLVIA: If he does, I'll assure you he shall never get to my heart. But can you have the conscience to love another man now you are married?

LADY DUNCE: I tell thee, Sylvia, I never was married to that Engine we have been talking of. My parents made me say something to him after a priest once but my heart went not along with my tongue. My thoughts, Sylvia, for these seven years have been much better employed. Beaugard! Ah, curse the day that sent him into France! Had he stayed here, I had not been sacrificed to the arms of this monument, for the bed of death could not be more cold than his has been. Beaugard would have delivered me from the monster for even then I loved him, and was apt to think my kindness not neglected.

SYLVIA: But how do you hope ever to get sight of him? Sir David's watchfulness is invincible. I dare swear he would smell out a rival if he were in the house by instinct as some sweat when a cat's in the room. Then again, Beaugard's a soldier and that's a thing the old gentleman, you know, loves dearly.

LADY DUNCE: There lies the greatest comfort of my uneasy life. He is one of those fools, forsooth, that are led by the nose by knaves to rail against the king. I have had hopes this twelvemonth to have heard of his being clapped in the Tower for treason.

SYLVIA: But I find only you are the prisoner all this while.

LADY DUNCE: At present indeed I am. But fortune, I hope, will smile wouldst thou be my friend, Sylvia.

SYLVIA: In any mischievous design, with all my heart.

LADY DUNCE: The conclusion, madam, may turn to your satisfaction. But have you no thoughts of Courtine?

SYLVIA: Not I, I assure you, cousin.

LADY DUNCE: You don't think him well-shaped, straight and proportionable?

SYLVIA: Considering he eats but once a week, the man is well enough.

LADY DUNCE: And then wears his clothes, you know, filthily and like a horrid sloven.

SYLVIA: Filthily enough with a threadbare red coat over which hangs a great, broad, greasy buff belt, enough to turn anyone's stomach, a peruke tied up in a knot to excuse its want of combing and then, because he has been a man-at-arms, he must wear two tuffles of a beard, forsooth, to lodge a dunghill of snuff upon to keep his nose in good humour.

LADY DUNCE: Nay, now I am sure that thou lovest him.

SYLVIA: So far from it that I protest eternally against the whole sex.

LADY DUNCE: That time will best demonstrate. In the meanwhile, to our business.

SYLVIA: As how, madam?

LADY DUNCE: Tonight I must see Beaugard. He and Courtine are this minute at dinner in the Haymarket. Now to make the evil genius that haunts me, my thing called husband, himself assist his poor wife would be not unpleasant.

SYLVIA: 'Twill be impossible.

LADY DUNCE: I am apt to be persuaded, 'twill be easy. You know our good and friendly neighbour, Sir Jolly.

SYLVIA: Out on him, the beast! He's always talking filthily to a body. If he sits but at the table he'll be making nasty figures in the napkins.

LADY DUNCE: He and my sweet yoke-fellow are the most intimate friends in the world so that, out of neighbourly kindness as well as the great delight he takes to be meddling in matters of this nature, with a great deal of pains and industry he has procured me Beaugard's picture and given Beaugard to understand how well a friend of his in petticoats, called myself, wishes him.

SYLVIA: But what's all this to making the husband instrumental?

LADY DUNCE: It must be done this night. I'll instantly to my chamber, take to my bed in a pet and send for Sir David.

SYLVIA: But which way then must the lover come?

LADY DUNCE: Nay, I'll betray Beaugard to him. I'll show him the picture, say it was sent to me by him and beg Sir Davy, as he values his own honour and my quiet, to secure me from this scandalous solicitation.

SYLVIA: And so make him the go-between.

LADY DUNCE: Right, Sylvia, 'tis the best office a husband can do a wife – I mean an old husband. Bless us! To be yoked in wedlock with a paralytic, coughing, decrepit dotterel! To be a dry nurse all one's lifetime to a child of sixty-five! To lie by the image of death a whole night, a dull immovable that has no sense of life but through its pains! The pigeon's as happy that's laid at a sick man's feet. For my part, this shall henceforth be my prayer:

Cursed be the memory, nay, double cursed
Of her that wedded age for interest first.
Worn bare with years, with fruitless wishes full,
He's all day troublesome and all night dull.
Who wed with fools indeed lead happy lives.
Fools are the fittest, finest things for wives.
Yet old men profit bring as fools bring ease
And both make youth and wit much better please.

ACT TWO

SCENE ONE

The Mall.

Enter SIR JOLLY JUMBLE, BEAUGARD, COURTINE and FOURBIN.

COURTINE: Sir Jolly is the glory of the age.

SIR JOLLY: Nay, now, sir, you honour me too far.

BEAUGARD: He's the delight of the young and the wonder of
the old.

SIR JOLLY: I swear, gentlemen, you make me blush.

COURTINE: He deserves a statue in gold at the charge of the
kingdom.

SIR JOLLY: Out upon't, fie for shame! I protest I'll leave your
company if you talk so. But, faith, they were pure whores,
daintily dutiful strumpets. Ha! Ud's-bud, they'd have
stripped for t'other bottle.

BEAUGARD: Truly, Sir Jolly, you are a man of very
extraordinary discipline. I never saw whores under better
command in my life.

SIR JOLLY: Pish, that's nothing, man, nothing. I can send for
forty better when I please, doxies that will skip, strip, leap,
trip and do anything in the world, anything, old soul.

COURTINE: Dear, dear Sir Jolly, where and when?

BEAUGARD: But, Sir Jolly, how goes my business forward?
When shall I have a view of the quarry I fly at?

SIR JOLLY: Alas-a-day, not so hasty. Soft and fair, I beseech
you. Ah, my little son of thunder, if thou hadst her in thy
arms now between a pair of sheets and I under the bed

to see fair play, boy, gemini, what would become of me? What would become of me? There would be doings! O lawd, I under the bed!

BEAUGARD: Or behind the hangings, Sir Jolly. Would not that do as well?

SIR JOLLY: Ah no. Under the bed, against the world. But then it would be very dark, ha!

BEAUGARD: Dark to choose.

SIR JOLLY: No, but a little light would do well, a small, glimmering lamp, just enough for me to steal a peep by. O lamentable! O lamentable! I won't speak a word more. There would be a trick! O rare, you friend, O rare! Od's so, not a word more, od's so! Yonder comes the monster that must be, the cuckold elect. Step aside and observe him. If I should be seen in your company 'twould spoil all.

Exeunt SIR JOLLY JUMBLE and COURTINE.

BEAUGARD: For my part, I'll stand the meeting of him. One way to promote a good understanding with a wife is first to get acquainted with her husband.

Enter SIR DAVY.

SIR DAVY: (*Aside.*) Well, of all blessings a discreet wife is the greatest that can light upon a man of years. Had I been married to anything but an angel now, what a beast had I been by this time! Well, I am the happiest old fool! 'Tis a horrid age we live in that an honest man can keep nothing to himself. If you have a good estate, every covetous rogue is longing for't. Truly, I love a good estate dearly myself. If you have a handsome wife, every smooth faced coxcomb will be combing and cocking at her. Flesh-flies are not so troublesome to the shambles as those sort of insects are to the boxes in the playhouse. But virtue is a great blessing, an invaluable treasure. To tell me herself that a villain had tempted her and give me the very picture, the enchantment he sent to bewitch her. It strikes me dumb with admiration. Here's the villain in effigy. (*Pulls out the picture.*) Od, a very handsome fellow, a dangerous rogue, I'll warrant him. Such fellows as these should be fettered like unruly colts that they might not leap into other men's pastures. Here's a nose I could find it in my heart to cut off. Damned dog, to dare to presume to make a cuckold of a knight! Bless us, what will this world come to! Well, poor Sir David, down, down, on thy knees (*Kneels.*) and thank thy stars for this deliverance.

BEAUGARD: 'Sdeath, what's that I see? 'Tis the very picture I sent by Sir Jolly. If so, by this light I am damnably jilted.

SIR DAVY: (*Aside.*) But now if –

BEAUGARD: Surely he does not see us yet.

FOURBIN: See you, sir? Why, he has but one eye and we are on his blind side. I'll dumbfound him.

FOURBIN strikes SIR DAVY on the shoulder.

SIR DAVY: (*Getting to his feet.*) Who the devil's this? Sir, sir, sir, who are you, sir?

BEAUGARD: (*Looking at the miniature in SIR DAVY's hand.*) Ay, ay, 'tis the same. Now a pox on all amorous adventures! 'Sdeath, I'll go beat the impertinent pimp that drew me into this fooling.

SIR DAVY: Sir, methinks you are very curious.

BEAUGARD: Sir, perhaps I have an extraordinary reason to be so.

SIR DAVY: And perhaps, sir, I care not for you nor for your reasons neither.

BEAUGARD: Sir, if you are at leisure, I would beg the honour to speak with you.

SIR DAVY: With me, sir? What's your business with me?

BEAUGARD: To be known to so worthy a person as you would be so extraordinary a happiness I could not avoid taking this opportunity of tendering you my service.

SIR DAVY: (*Aside.*) Smooth rogue! Who the devil is this fellow? (*To BEAUGARD.*) But, sir, you were pleased to nominate business, sir. I desire with what speed you can to know your business that I may go about my business.

BEAUGARD: Sir, if I might with good manners, I should be glad to inform myself whose picture that is which you have in your hand. Methinks it is very fine painting.

SIR DAVY: Picture, friend, picture? Sir, 'tis the resemblance of a very impudent fellow. They call him Captain Beaugard, forsooth. But he is in short a rakehell, a poor, lousy, beggarly, disbanded devil. Do you know him, friend?

BEAUGARD: I think I have heard of such a vagabond. The truth of't is he is a very impudent fellow.

SIR DAVY: Ay, a damned rogue.

BEAUGARD: O, a notorious scoundrel!

SIR DAVY: I expect to hear he's hanged by next sessions.

BEAUGARD: The truth of't is he has deserved it long ago. But did you ever see him, Sir David?

SIR DAVY: (*Aside.*) Sir – ? Does he know me?

BEAUGARD: Because I fancy that miniature is very like him. Pray, sir, whence had it you?

SIR DAVY: Had it, friend? Whence had it I? (*Compares the picture with BEAUGARD's face. Aside.*) Bless us! What have I done now! This is the very traitor himself. If he should be desperate and put his sword in my guts! Slitting my nose will be as bad. I have but one eye left and may be – oh, but this is the king's court. Od, that's well remembered. He dares not but be civil here. I'll try to outhuff him. (*To BEAUGARD.*) 'Whence had it you?'

BEAUGARD: Ay, sir, whence had it you? That's English in my country, sir.

SIR DAVY: Go, sir, you are a rascal.

BEAUGARD: How?

SIR DAVY: Sir, I say you are a rascal, a very impudent rascal. Nay, I'll prove you to be a rascal if you go to that.

BEAUGARD: Sir, I am a gentleman and a soldier.

SIR DAVY: So much the worse. Soldiers have been cuckold-makers from the beginning. Sir, I care not what you are. For aught I know, you may be a – come, sir, did I never see you? Answer me to that. Did I never see you? For aught I know, you may be a Jesuit. To my knowledge, there were several at Hounslow Heath disguised in dirty petticoats and cried, 'Brandy!' I knew a sergeant that was familiar with one of 'em all night in a ditch and fancied him a woman. But the devil is powerful.

BEAUGARD: In short, you worthy villain of worship, that picture is mine and I must have it or I shall take an opportunity to kick your worship most inhumanly.

SIR DAVY: Kick, sir?

BEAUGARD: Ay, sir, kick. 'Tis a recreation I can show you.

SIR DAVY: Sir, I am a free-born subject of England and there are laws, look you, there are laws. So I say you are a rascal again and now how will you help yourself? Poor fool!

BEAUGARD: Hark you, friend, have not you a wife?

SIR DAVY: I have a lady, sir. O, and she's mightily taken with this picture of yours. She was so mightily proud of it, she could not forbear showing it me and telling me too who 'twas sent it her.

BEAUGARD: And has she been long a jilt? Has she practised the trade for any time?

SIR DAVY: Trade! Humph, what trade? What trade, friend?

BEAUGARD: Why, the trade of whore and no whore – caterwauling in jest, putting out Christian colours when she's a Turk under deck. A curse upon all honest women in the flesh that are whores in the spirit.

SIR DAVY: (*Aside.*) Poor devil! How he rails! Ha, ha, ha! (*To BEAUGARD.*) Look you, sweet soul, as I told you, there are laws. But those are things not worthy your consideration. Beauty's your business. But, dear vagabond, trouble thyself no further about my spouse. Let my doxy rest in peace. She's meat for thy master, old boy. I have my belly full of her every night.

BEAUGARD: Sir, I wish all your noble family hanged, from the bottom of my heart.

SIR DAVY: Moreover, Captain, I must tell you my wife is one that I have loved from her infancy and she deserves it for she has discovered loyally to me the treacherous designs laid against her chastity and my honour.

BEAUGARD: By this light, the beast weeps.

SIR DAVY: Truly, I cannot but weep for joy to think how happy I am in a sincere, faithful and loving yoke-fellow. She charged me to tell you into the bargain that she is sufficiently satisfied of the most secret wishes of your heart.

BEAUGARD: I am glad of't.

SIR DAVY: And that 'tis her desire that you would trouble yourself no more about the matter.

BEAUGARD: With all my heart.

SIR DAVY: But henceforward behave yourself with such discretion as becomes a gentleman.

BEAUGARD: O, to be sure, most exactly!

SIR DAVY: And let her alone to make the best use of those innocent freedoms I allow her without putting her reputation in hazard.

BEAUGARD: As how, I beseech you?

SIR DAVY: By your impertinent and unseasonable address.

BEAUGARD: And this news you bring me by particular commission of your sweet lady?

SIR DAVY: Yea, dear heart, I do and she hopes you'll be sensible of her good meaning by it. These were her very words. I neither add nor diminish.

BEAUGARD: Then all the curses I shall think on this twelvemonth light on her – and as many more on the next fool that gives credit to her sex.

SIR DAVY: (*Aside.*) Well, certainly I am the happiest toad! How melancholy the monkey stands now! Poor pug, hast thou lost her?

BEAUGARD: (*Aside.*) To be so sordid a jilt, to betray me to such a beast as that! Can she have any good thoughts of such a swine? Damn her!

SIR DAVY: Now, sir, with your permission I'll take my leave.

BEAUGARD: Sir, if you were gone to the devil I should think you well disposed of.

SIR DAVY: If you have any letter or other commendation to the lady that was so charmed with your resemblance, it shall be very faithfully conveyed by –

BEAUGARD: Fool!

SIR DAVY: Your humble servant, sir. I'm gone. I shall disturb you no further. Your most humble servant, sir

Exit SIR DAVY.

BEAUGARD: Now poverty, plague, pox and prison fall thick upon the head of thee! Fourbin!

FOURBIN: Sir!

BEAUGARD: Thou hast been an extraordinary rogue in thy time.

FOURBIN: I hope I have lost nothing in your honour's service, sir.

BEAUGARD: Find out some way to revenge me on this old rascal and if I do not make thee a gentleman –

FOURBIN: That you have been pleased to do long ago for I am sure you have not put one shilling in my pocket.

BEAUGARD: (*Giving FOURBIN money.*) Here, for thee to revel with.

FOURBIN: Will your honour please to have his throat cut?

BEAUGARD: With all my heart.

FOURBIN: Or would you have him decently hanged at his own door and give out to the world he did it himself?

BEAUGARD: Excellent, Fourbin.

FOURBIN: Leave matters to my discretion and if I do not –

BEAUGARD: Thou wilt, I know. Go about it, prosper and be famous.

Exit FOURBIN.

Now ere I dare venture to meet Courtine will I go by myself, rail for an hour and then be better company.

SCENE TWO

Still the Mall.

Enter COURTINE and SYLVIA.

SYLVIA: Take my word, sir, you had better give this business over. I tell you there's nothing in the world turns my stomach so much as the man that makes love to me. I never saw one of your sex in my life make love but he looked so like an ass all the while I blushed for him.

COURTINE: I am afraid your ladyship is one of those dangerous creatures who are so mightily taken with admiring themselves nothing else is worth their notice.

SYLVIA: O, who can be so dull as not to be ravished by that roisterous visage of yours? That ruffling air in your gait that seems to cry where'er you go, 'Make room, here comes the captain'? That face which bids defiance to the weather. Bless us! If I were a poor farmer's wife in the country and you wanted quarters, how would it aim to fright me! But as I am young and not very ugly, how lovingly it looks upon me.

COURTINE: Who can forbear to sigh, look pale and languish where beauty and wit unite to enslave a heart so tractable as mine? First, for that modish swim of your body, the victorious motion of your arms and head, the glancing of the eyes. Bless us! If I were a dainty, fine-dressed coxcomb with a great estate and a little or no wit, vanity in abundance and good for nothing, how would they melt and soften me! But as I am a scandalous honest rascal, not fool enough to be your sport nor rich enough to be your prey, how gloatingly they look upon me!

SYLVIA: Well, the more I look, the more I'm in love with you.

COURTINE: The more I look, the more I am out of love with you.

SYLVIA: How my heart swells when I see you!

COURTINE: How my stomach rises when I'm near you!

SYLVIA: Nay, then let's bargain.

COURTINE: With all my heart. What?

SYLVIA: Not to fall in love with each other, I assure you, Monsieur Captain.

COURTINE: But to hate one another constantly and cordially.

SYLVIA: Always when you are drunk I desire you to talk scandalously of me.

COURTINE: Ay, and when I am sober too. In return whereof, whene'er you see a coquette of your acquaintance and I be named, be sure you spit at the filthy remembrance and rail at me as if you loved me.

SYLVIA: Whene'er we meet in the Mall I desire you to humph, put out your tongue, make ugly mouths, laugh aloud and look back at me.

COURTINE: Which if I do, be sure at the next turning to pick up some tawdry fluttering fop to saunter by your side with his hat under his arm.

SYLVIA: Harkening to all the bitter things I say to be revenged. Counterfeit sweet letters from me.

COURTINE: And you, to be even with me for the scandal, publish to all the world I offered to marry you.

SYLVIA: O hideous marriage!

COURTINE: Horrid, horrid marriage!

SYLVIA: Name no more of it.

COURTINE: At that sad word let's part.

SYLVIA: Let's wish all men decrepit, dull and silly.

COURTINE: And every woman old and ugly.

SYLVIA: Adieu!

COURTINE: Farewell!

Enter FRISK, a young fellow affectedly dressed.

SYLVIA: Ah me, Mr Frisk!

FRISK: Mademoiselle Sylvia! Sincerely, as I hope to be saved, the devil take me, damn me, madam, who's that?

SYLVIA: Ha, ha, ha, ha!

Exit SYLVIA with FRISK.

COURTINE: True to thy failings always, woman! How naturally is thy sex fond of a rogue! What a monster was that for a woman to delight in! Now must I love her still though I know I am a blockhead for't. What's to be done? I'll have three whores a day to keep love out of my head.

Enter BEAUGARD.

Beaugard, well met! How go matters? Handsomely?

BEAUGARD: O very handsomely! Had you but seen how handsomely I was used just now you would swear so. I have heard thee rail in my time. Would thou wouldst exercise thy talent at present.

COURTINE: At what?

BEAUGARD: Why, canst thou ever want a subject! Rail at thyself, rail at me. I deserve to be railed at.

A clumsy fellow marches over the stage dressed like an officer.

See there! What think'st thou of that engine, that moving lump of filthiness miscalled a man?

COURTINE: Curse him for a rogue! I know him.

BEAUGARD: So.

COURTINE: That rascal was a retailer of ale but yesterday and now he is an officer. Be hanged! 'Tis a dainty sight of a morning to see him march, his toes turned in, drawing his legs after him, at the head of a hundred lusty fellows. Some honest gentleman or other stays at home because that dog had money to bribe some corrupt colonel.

Enter another, gravely dressed.

BEAUGARD: There's another of my acquaintance. He was my father's footman not long since and has pimped for me oftener than he prayed for himself. That quality recommended him to a nobleman's service which, together with flattering, fawning, lying, spying and informing, has raised him to an employment of trust and reputation though the rogue can't write his name.

COURTINE: 'Tis as unreasonable to expect a man of sense to get on in the world as to think a priest can be religious, a fair woman chaste or a pardoned rebel loyal.

Enter two more, seeming earnestly in discourse.

BEAUGARD: That's seasonably thought on. Look there. Observe that fellow on the right hand, the rogue with the busiest face of the two. I'll tell thee his history.

COURTINE: I hope hanging will be the end of his history, so well I like him at first sight.

BEAUGARD: He was born a vagabond and no parish owned him. His father was as obscure as his mother public. Everybody knew her and nobody could guess at him.

COURTINE: He comes of a very good family, heaven be praised.

BEAUGARD: The thing he chose to rise by was rebellion. So a rebel he grew and flourished a rebel, fought against his king and helped bring him to the block. In short, he was persecutor-general of a whole county by which he got enough, at the new king's return, to secure for himself a pardon.

COURTINE: Nauseous vermin! That such swine with the mark of rebellion on their forehead should wallow in luxury whilst honest men are forgotten! What a dreadful beard and swinging sword he wears!

BEAUGARD: He will endure kicking most temperately for all that. I know five or six more of the same stamp that never come abroad without terrible long spits by their sides with which they will let you, if you please, bore their own noses!

COURTINE: But, friend Beaugard, methinks thou art very splenetic of a sudden. How goes the affair of love forward? Prosperously, ha?

BEAUGARD: O, I assure you, most triumphantly. Just now, you must know, I am parted with the sweet, civil, enchanted lady's husband.

COURTINE: Well, and what says the cuckold? Is he very kind and good-natured as cuckolds ought to be?

BEAUGARD: Why, he says, Courtine, in short, that I am a very silly fellow – and truly I am very apt to believe him – and that I have been jilted in this affair most unconscionably. A plague on all pimps, say I! A man's business never thrives so well as when he is his own solicitor.

Enter SIR JOLLY JUMBLE.

SIR JOLLY: (*To BEAUGARD.*) Hist, hist, captain, captain, captain. Here's luck, here's luck. Now or never, captain, never if not now, Captain! Here's luck.

BEAUGARD: Sir Jolly, no more adventures, sweet Sir Jolly. I am like to have a very fine time of't, truly.

SIR JOLLY: The best in the world, dear dog, the very best in the world. 'Sbud, she's here hard by, man, stays on purpose for thee, finely disguised. The cuckold has lost her and nobody knows anything of the matter but I, nobody but I and I, you must know, I am I, ha! And I, you little toad, ha –

BEAUGARD: You are a very fine gentleman.

SIR JOLLY: The best-natured fellow in the world, I believe, of my years! Now does my heart so thump for fear this business should miscarry. Why, I'll warrant thee, the lady is here, man. She's all thy own. 'Tis thy own fault if thou art not in *terra incognita* within this half-hour. Come along, prithee come along. Fie for shame! What, make a lady lose her longing! Come along, I say, you – out upon't!

BEAUGARD: Sir, your humble. I shan't, sir.

SIR JOLLY: What? Not go?

BEAUGARD: No, sir, no lady for me.

SIR JOLLY: Not go! I should laugh at that, faith.

BEAUGARD: No, I will assure you. Not go, sir.

SIR JOLLY: Away, you wag. You jest, you jest, you wag. 'Not go', quotha?

BEAUGARD: No, sir, not go, I tell you. What the devil would you have more?

SIR JOLLY: Nothing, nothing, sir, but I am a gentleman.

BEAUGARD: With all my heart.

SIR JOLLY: And do you think that I'll be used thus?

BEAUGARD: Sir!

SIR JOLLY: Take away my reputation and take away my life. I shall be disgraced forever.

BEAUGARD: I have not wronged you, Sir Jolly.

SIR JOLLY: Not wronged me! But you shall find you have wronged me and wronged a sweet lady and a fine lady. I shall never be trusted again, never have employment more! I shall die of the spleen. Prithee now be good-natured, be persuaded. Od, I'll give thee this ring. I'll give thee this watch – 'tis gold. I'll give thee anything in the world. Go!

BEAUGARD: Not one foot, sir.

SIR JOLLY: (*Aside.*) Now that I durst but murder him. Well, shall I fetch her to thee? What shall I do for thee?

Enter LADY DUNCE.

Od's fish, here she comes herself. Now, you ill-natured churl, now, you devil, look upon her, do but look upon her. What shall I say to her?

BEAUGARD: What you please, Sir Jolly.

SIR JOLLY: (*Aside.*) 'Tis a very strange monster, this. (*Goes to LADY DUNCE.*) Madam, this is the gentleman. That's he.

Though, as one may say, he's something bashful but I'll tell him who you are. (*Goes to BEAUGARD.*) If thou art not more cruel than leopards, lions, tigers, wolves or Tartars, don't break my heart, don't kill me. This unkindness goes to the soul of me. (*Goes to LADY DUNCE.*) Madam, he says he's so amazed at your triumphant beauty that he dares not approach the excellence that shines from you.

LADY DUNCE: (*Aside.*) What can be the meaning of all this?

SIR JOLLY: (*To BEAUGARD.*) Art thou resolved to be remorseless? Canst thou be insensible? Hast thou eyes? Hast thou a heart? Hast thou anything thou shouldst have? Od, I'll tickle thee. Get you to her, you fool, get you to her, to her, to her, to her. Ha, ha, ha.

LADY DUNCE: Have you forgot me, Beaugard?

SIR JOLLY: (*To BEAUGARD.*) So, now, to her again I say, to her, to her and be hanged. Ah rogue, ah rogue! Now, now, have at her, now have at her.

SIR JOLLY propels BEAUGARD towards LADY DUNCE.

There it goes, there it goes. Hey, boys!

LADY DUNCE: Methinks this face should not so much be altered as to be nothing like what once I thought it – the object of your pleasure and the subject of your praises.

SIR JOLLY: (*Aside.*) Cunning toad! Wheedling jade! You shall see now how by degrees she'll draw him into the whirlpool of love. Now he leers upon her, now he leers upon her. O law! There's eyes! There's your eyes! I must pinch him by the calf of the leg.

BEAUGARD: Madam, I must confess I do remember that I had once acquaintance with a face whose air and beauty much resembled yours. If I may trust my heart, you are called Clarinda.

LADY DUNCE: Clarinda I was called till my ill fortune wedded me. Now you may have heard of me by another tide. Your friend has, I suppose, made nothing a secret to you.

BEAUGARD: And are you then that kind, enchanted, fair one who was so passionately in love with my picture that you could not forbear betraying me to the beast your husband, wronging the passion of one that languished only to make your monster merry? Hark you, madam. Had your fool been worth it, I had beaten him and have a mind to exercise my parts that way upon your go-between, your male bawd there.

SIR JOLLY: (*Aside.*) Ah Lord, ah Lord! All's spoiled, all's ruined. I shall be undone forever. Why, what a devil is the matter now? What sins have I committed?

LADY DUNCE: And are you that passionate adorer of our sex who cannot live a week in London without loving? Are you the spark that sends your picture up and down to longing ladies, longing for a pattern of your person?

BEAUGARD: Yes, madam, when I receive so good hostages as these (*Shows the gold.*) that it shall be well used. Could you find out nobody but me to play the fool with?

SIR JOLLY: (*Aside.*) Alack-a-day!

LADY DUNCE: Could you pitch upon nobody but that wretched woman that loved you too well to abuse you thus?

SIR JOLLY: (*Aside.*) That ever I was born!

BEAUGARD: Here, here, madam, I'll return you your dirt. (*Attempts to return the money.*) I scorn your wages as I do your service.

LADY DUNCE: Fie for shame! What, refund? That is not like a soldier. Keep it to pay your seamstress.

SIR JOLLY: (*Aside.*) His seamstress! Who the devil is his seamstress? Od, what would I give to know that now?

LADY DUNCE: There was a ring too which I sent you this afternoon. If that fit not your finger, dispose of it where it may give no occasion of scandal and you'll do well.

BEAUGARD: A ring, madam!

LADY DUNCE: A small trifle. I suppose Sir David delivered it to you when he returned your miniature?

BEAUGARD: I beseech you, madam –

LADY DUNCE: Farewell, traitor.

BEAUGARD: As I hope to be saved –

LADY DUNCE: Go! You are a false, ungrateful brute. Trouble me no more.

Exit LADY DUNCE.

BEAUGARD: Sir Jolly, Sir Jolly, Sir Jolly –

SIR JOLLY: Ah, thou rebel!

BEAUGARD: Some advice, dear friend, ere I'm ruined.

SIR JOLLY: Twopennyworth of hemp for your honour's supper, that's all the remedy I know.

BEAUGARD: Prithee hear a little reason.

SIR JOLLY: No, sir, I ha' done. No more to be said. I am ashamed of you. I have no more to say to you. I'll never see your face again. Good-bye.

Exit SIR JOLLY JUMBLE.

BEAUGARD: Death and the devil, what have my stars been doing today? A ring! Delivered by Sir David! What can that mean? Pox on her for a jilt! She lies and has a mind to laugh at me a day or two longer. Hist, here comes her beast once more. I'll use him civilly and try what discovery I can make.

Enter SIR DAVY.

SIR DAVY: (*Aside.*) Ha, ha, ha! Here's the captain's jewel. Very well. In troth, I had forgotten it. Ha, ha, ha! How damnably mad he'll be when I shall deliver him his ring again. Ha, ha! Poor dog, he'll hang himself at least. Ha, ha, ha! Faith, 'tis a very pretty stone and finely set. Humph, if I should keep it now! I'll say I lost it. No, I'll give it him o' purpose to vex him. Ha, ha, ha!

BEAUGARD: (*Doffing his hat.*) Sir David, I am heartily sorry.

SIR DAVY: O sir, 'tis you I was seeking for. Ha, ha, ha! (*Aside.*) What shall I say to him now to terrify him?

BEAUGARD: Me, sir?

SIR DAVY: Ay, you, sir, if your name be Captain Beaugard. (*Aside.*) How like a fool he looks already!

BEAUGARD: What you please, sir.

SIR DAVY: Sir, I should speak a word with you, if you think fit. (*Aside.*) What shall I do now to keep my countenance?

BEAUGARD: Can I be so happy, sir, as to be able to serve you in anything?

SIR DAVY: No, sir – ha, ha, ha! – I have commands of service to you, sir. O Lord! Ha, ha, ha!

BEAUGARD: Me, sir?

SIR DAVY: Ay, sir, you, sir. But put on your hat, friend, put on your hat, be covered.

BEAUGARD: Sir, will you please to sit down on this bank?

SIR DAVY: No, no, there's no need, no need. For all I have a young wife, I can stand upon my legs, sweetheart. I think, friend, we had some hard words just now. 'Twas about a paltry baggage but she's a pretty baggage and a witty baggage and a baggage that –

BEAUGARD: Sir, I am heartily ashamed of all misdemeanour on my side.

SIR DAVY: You do well. Though are not you a damned whoremaster, a devilish, cuckold-making fellow? Here, here, do you see this? Here's the ring you sent a-roguing. Sir, do you think my wife wants anything you can help her to? Why, I'll warrant this ring cost fifty pound. What a prodigal fellow are you to throw away so much money? Or didst thou steal it, old boy? I believe thou may'st be poor. I'll lend thee money upon't, if thou think'st fit, because I love thee. Ha, ha, ha!

BEAUGARD: Sir, your humble servant. I am sorry 'twas not worth your lady's acceptance. (*Aside.*) Now what a dog am I!

SIR DAVY: I should have given it thee before but, faith, I forgot it. It was not my wife's fault in the least for she says if thou like'st this usage she hopes to have thy custom again, child. Ha, ha, ha!

BEAUGARD: Then, sir, I beseech you tell her you have made a convert of me and I am so sensible of my insolent behaviour towards her –

SIR DAVY: Very well, I shall do it.

BEAUGARD: That 'tis impossible I shall ever be at peace with myself till I find some way to make her reparation.

SIR DAVY: Very good. Ha, ha, ha!

BEAUGARD: And that if ever she find me guilty of the like offence again –

SIR DAVY: No, sir, you had best not. But proceed. Ha, ha, ha!

BEAUGARD: Let her banish all good opinion of me forever.

SIR DAVY: No more to be said. Your servant. Good-bye.

BEAUGARD: One word more, I beseech you, Sir Davy.

SIR DAVY: What's that?

BEAUGARD: I beg you tell her that the reproof she has given me has so wrought upon me –

SIR DAVY: Well, I will.

BEAUGARD: That I esteem this jewel not merely as a wreck redeemed from my folly but that for her sake I will preserve it to the utmost moment of my life.

SIR DAVY: With all my heart, I vow and swear.

BEAUGARD: And that I long to convince her I am not the brute she mistook me for.

SIR DAVY: Right. Let me see. First you acknowledge yourself to be a very impudent fellow.

BEAUGARD: I do, sir.

SIR DAVY: And that you shall never be at rest till you have satisfied my lady.

BEAUGARD: Right, sir!

SIR DAVY: Satisfied her! Very good. Ha, ha, ha! And that you will never play the fool anymore.

BEAUGARD: Never, sir.

SIR DAVY: And that you will keep that ring for her sake as long as you live, ha!

BEAUGARD: To the day of my death, I assure you.

SIR DAVY: And that you long, mightily long, to let her understand you are quite another fellow than that she takes you for.

BEAUGARD: Exactly, sir. That is the sum and end of my desires.

SIR DAVY: Well, I'll take care of your business, I warrant you. (*Aside.*) This will make the purest sport when I come home – no? (*To BEAUGARD.*) Well, your servant.

Exit SIR DAVY.

BEAUGARD: So, now I find a husband is a delicate instrument if rightly made use of. To make her old, jealous coxcomb pimp for me himself!

Ah, were ye all such husbands and such wives,
We younger sons should lead far better lives.

ACT THREE

SCENE ONE

Covent Garden.

Enter SYLVIA and COURTINE from different directions.

SYLVIA: (*Aside.*) To fall in love and to fall in love with a soldier! Nay, a disbanded soldier too, a fellow with the mark of Cain upon him which everybody knows him by and is ready to throw stones at him for.

COURTINE: (*Aside.*) Damn her! I shall never enjoy her without ravishing. If she were but very rich and very ugly, I would marry her. (*Seeing SYLVIA.*) Ay, 'tis she. I know her mischievous look too well to be mistaken. Madam!

SYLVIA: Sir.

COURTINE: 'Tis a very hard case that you have resolved not to let me be quiet.

SYLVIA: 'Tis very unreasonably done of you, sir, to haunt me up and down at this scandalous rate. The world will think we are acquainted shortly.

COURTINE: So, madam, I shall take more care of my reputation and from this time forward shun and avoid you most watchfully.

SYLVIA: Have you not haunted this place these two hours?

COURTINE: 'Twas because I knew it to be your ladyship's home and therefore might reasonably be the place you least of all frequented. One would imagine you were gone a-coxcomb-hunting by this time to some place of public appearance. 'Twill be twilight presently and then the owls come all abroad.

SYLVIA: What need I take the trouble to go so far a-fowling when there's game enough at our own doors?

COURTINE: What, game for your net, fair lady?

SYLVIA: Yes, or any woman's net that will spread it.

COURTINE: To show you how despicably I think of the business I will leave you, though I lose the pleasure of railing at you.

SYLVIA: Do so. Your raillery betrays your wit as badly as your clumsy civility your breeding.

COURTINE: Adieu!

SYLVIA: Farewell!

COURTINE: Why do not you go about your business?

SYLVIA: Because I would be sure to be rid of you first that you might not dog me.

COURTINE: Were it possible that you could answer me one question truly I should be satisfied.

SYLVIA: Anything to be rid of you.

COURTINE: Are you honest? Look in my face and tell me.

SYLVIA: Look in your face? For what? To spoil my stomach for my supper?

COURTINE: No, to get thee a stomach to thy bed, sweetheart. I would be better acquainted with thee because thou art very ill-natured.

SYLVIA: Your only way to bring that business about is to be more troublesome and if you think it worth your while to be abused, you may make your personal appearance this night.

COURTINE: How? Where? When? At what hour, I beseech thee?

SYLVIA: Under the window between the hours of eleven and twelve exactly.

COURTINE: And shall these lovely eyes and ears
Hear my plaints and see my tears?

SYLVIA: At that kind hour thy griefs shall end
If thou canst know thy foe from thy friend.

Exit SYLVIA.

COURTINE: Here's another trick of the devil now! Under that window between the hours of eleven and twelve exactly! I am a damned fool and must go. Let me see. Suppose I meet with a lusty beating! Pish, that's nothing for a man in love. Or suppose she contrive some way to make a public coxcomb of me and expose me to the scorn of the world for an example to all amorous blockheads hereafter? Why, if she do, I'll swear I have lain with her, beat her relations if they attempt to vindicate her. So there's one love intrigue pretty well over.

SCENE TWO

Still Covent Garden.

Enter SIR DAVY and VERMIN.

SIR DAVY: Go, get you in to your lady now and tell her I am coming.

VERMIN: Her ladyship, right-worshipful, is pleased not to be at home.

SIR DAVY: How's that? My lady not at home! Run in and ask when she went forth, whither she is gone and who is with her. Run and ask, Vermin.

VERMIN: She went out in her chair this afternoon.

SIR DAVY: Then I may be a cuckold. What will become of me? I have surely lost and ne'er shall find her more. She promised me strictly to stay at home till I came back again. For aught I know she may be taking the air as far as Knightsbridge with some smooth faced rogue. 'Tis a damned house, that Swan. That Swan at Knightsbridge is a confounded house, Vermin.

VERMIN: Do you think she is there?

SIR DAVY: Would that Barn Elms was under water too. There's a thousand cuckolds a year made at Barn Elms by Rosamond's Ponds. The devil! If she should be there this evening, my heart's broke.

Enter SIR JOLLY JUMBLE.

SIR JOLLY: (*Aside.*) That must be Sir Davy. Ay, that's he, that's he. Ha, ha, ha! Was ever the like heard of? Was ever anything so pleasant?

SIR DAVY: I'll lock her up three days and three nights without meat, drink or light. I'll humble her in the devil's name.

SIR JOLLY: (*Pretending to search for SIR DAVY.*) Well, could I but meet my friend Sir Davy, it would be the joyfullest news for him.

SIR DAVY: Who's there that has anything to say to me?

SIR JOLLY: Ah my friend of friends, such news, such tidings.

SIR DAVY: I have lost my wife, man.

SIR JOLLY: Lost her! She's not dead, I hope.

SIR DAVY: Yes, alas, she's dead, irrecoverably lost.

SIR JOLLY: Why, I parted with her within this half-hour.

SIR DAVY: Did you so? Are you sure it was she? Where was it? I'll have my Lord Chief Justice's warrant and a constable.

SIR JOLLY: She made the purest sport with a young fellow, man, that she met with accidentally.

SIR DAVY: O Lord! Worse and worse. My wife making sport with a young fellow! Here are doings! I'll run mad. I'll climb Bow steeple, bestride the dragon and preach cuckoldom to the whole city.

SIR JOLLY: But best of all was that the coxcomb that claimed to be in love with her was a rascal.

SIR DAVY: In love with her! Who was it? What's his name? I warrant you, I won't tell a body. I'll indict him in the Crown Office. No, I'll issue warrants to apprehend him for treason upon the statute of Edward the Nineteenth. Won't you tell me what young fellow it was? Was it a very handsome young fellow, ha?

SIR JOLLY: Handsome? Yes, hang him. The fellow's handsome enough. He is not very handsome neither but he has a devilish leering black eye.

SIR DAVY: O Lord!

SIR JOLLY: His face too is a good riding face. 'Tis no soft, effeminate complexion. His countenance is ruddy, sanguine and cheerful. A devilish fellow in a corner, I'll warrant him.

SIR DAVY: Bless us, what will become of me! Why the devil did I marry a young wife? Is he very well-shaped too, tall, straight and proportionable, ha?

SIR JOLLY: Tall? No, he's not very tall neither. Yet he is tall enough too. He's your true English breed – well-knit, able and fit for service, old boy. Well-shaped, very well-proportioned, strong and active. I have seen the rogue leap like a buck.

SIR DAVY: Who can this be? And what think you, friend? Has he been there? Come, come, I'm sensible she's a young woman and I an old fellow, troth a very old fellow. I signify little or nothing now. Do you think he has prevailed? Am I a cuckold, neighbour?

SIR JOLLY: Cuckold? What! A cuckold in Covent Garden? No, I assure you, I believe her to be the most virtuous woman in the world. If you had but seen!

SIR DAVY: Ay, would I had! What was it?

SIR JOLLY: How like a rogue she used him. First of all up comes the spark to her. 'Madam,' says he and then he bows down thus. 'How now,' says she, 'what would this impertinent fellow have?'

SIR DAVY: Humph! Ha! Well, and what then?

SIR JOLLY: 'Madam', says he again bowing as he did before, 'my heart is so entirely yours that unless you take pity of my sufferings I must die here at your feet.'

SIR DAVY: So, and what said she again, neighbour? Ha!

SIR JOLLY: 'Go, go, go, you are a fop.'

SIR DAVY: Ha, ha, ha! Did she indeed? Did she say so indeed? I am glad of't, troth I am very glad of't. Well, and what next? And how, and well, and what? Ha!

SIR JOLLY: 'Madam,' says he, 'this won't do. I am your humble servant for all this. You may pretend to be as ill-natured as you please but I shall make bold.'

SIR DAVY: Was there ever such an impudent fellow?

SIR JOLLY: With that, 'Sirrah,' says she, 'you are a saucy jackanapes and I'll have you kicked.'

SIR DAVY: Ha, ha, ha! Well, I would not be unmarried again to be an angel.

SIR JOLLY: But the best jest of all was who this should be at last.

SIR DAVY: Ay, who indeed? I'll warrant you, some silly fellow or other. Poor fool!

SIR JOLLY: E'en a scandalous rakehell that lingers up and down the town by the name of Captain Beaugard.

SIR DAVY: Beaugard! Hang him, sot. Is it he? I don't value him thus, not a wet finger, man. To my knowledge she hates him, she scorns him, neighbour. I know it. I am very well satisfied on that point. Besides, I have seen him since and outhectored him. I am to tell her from his own mouth that he promises never to affront her more.

SIR JOLLY: Indeed?

SIR DAVY: Ay, ay.

Enter LADY DUNCE.

SIR JOLLY: (*To SIR DAVY.*) Hush, hush, there's my lady. I'll be gone. I'll not be seen. Your humble servant. Good-bye.

SIR DAVY: No, faith, Sir Jolly, go into my house now and stay supper with me. We han't supped together a great while.

SIR JOLLY: Ha! Say you so? I don't care if I do. Faith, with all my heart. (*Aside.*) This may give me opportunity to set all things right again.

SIR DAVY: My dear!

LADY DUNCE: Sir!

SIR DAVY: You have been abroad, my dear, I see.

LADY DUNCE: Only for a little air. Truly, I was almost stifled within doors. I hope you will not be angry, Sir David, will you?

SIR DAVY: Angry, child! No, child, not I. What should I be angry for?

LADY DUNCE: I wonder, Sir David, you will serve me at this rate. Did you not promise me to go in my behalf to Beaugard and correct him for his insolence according to my instructions?

SIR DAVY: So I did, child. I have been with him, sweetheart. I have told him all to a tittle. I gave him back the picture too but, as the devil would have it, I forgot the ring.

LADY DUNCE: Did you purpose, Sir Sodom, to render me ridiculous to the man I abominate? What scandalous interpretation, think you, must he make of my retaining any trifle of his sent me on so dishonourable terms?

SIR DAVY: Really, my lamb, thou art in the right. Yet I went back afterwards, dear heart, and did the business to some purpose.

LADY DUNCE: I am glad you did, with all my heart.

SIR DAVY: I gave him his lesson, I'll warrant him.

LADY DUNCE: Lesson? What lesson had you to give him?

SIR DAVY: Why, I told him if he liked the usage he had from you, he might come again for more. Ha, ha, ha!

LADY DUNCE: Ay, and so let him.

SIR DAVY: With all my heart. I'll give him free leave or hang me. Though thou wouldst not imagine how the poor devil's altered. La you there now! But as certain as I stand here, that man is so troubled he swears he shall not rest day nor night till he has satisfied thee. Prithee be satisfied with him if 'tis possible, my dear, prithee do. I promised him before I left to tell thee as much for the poor wretch looks so simply I could not choose but pity him, I vow and swear. Ha, ha, ha!

SIR JOLLY: (*Aside.*) Now, now, you little witch, now, you chits face! Od, I could find in my heart to put my little finger in your bubbies.

LADY DUNCE: Sir David, I must tell you that I cannot but resent your so soon reconcilement with a man I hate worse than death, and that if you love me with half the tenderness you profess, you would not forget an affront so palpably and so basely offered me.

SIR DAVY: Why, chicken, where's the remedy? What's to be done? How wouldst thou have me deal with him?

LADY DUNCE: Cut his throat.

SIR DAVY: Bless us forever! Cut his throat? What, do murder?

LADY DUNCE: Murder? Yes, anything to such an incorrigible enemy of your honour. See here this letter. This I received since I last parted with you. Just now it was thrown into my chair by an impudent lackey of his, kept o' purpose for such employment.

SIR DAVY: Let me see. A letter indeed! (*Reads.*) 'For the Lady Dunce.' Damned rogue, treacherous dog! What can he say in the inside now? Here's a villain.

SIR DAVY starts to open the letter.

LADY DUNCE: Yes, you had best break it open, you had so. 'Tis like the rest of your discretion.

SIR DAVY: Lady, if I have an enemy it is best for me to know what mischief he intends me. Therefore, with your leave, I will break it open.

LADY DUNCE: Do, do, to have him believe that I was so pleased with it as to do it myself. If you have the spirit of a gentleman in you, carry it back and dash it as it is in the face of that audacious fellow.

SIR JOLLY: (*Aside.*) What can be the meaning of this now?

SIR DAVY: A gentleman, yes, madam, I am a gentleman and the world shall find I am a gentleman. (*Aside.*) I have certainly the best woman in the world.

LADY DUNCE: What do you think will be the end of all this? I have no refuge in the world but your kindness. Had I a jealous husband, how miserable must my life be!

SIR JOLLY: (*Aside.*) Ah rogue's nose! Ah devil! Ah toad! Cunning thief, wheedling slut! I'll bite her by and by.

SIR DAVY: Poor fool! No, dear, I am not jealous nor never will be jealous of thee. Do what thou wilt, thou shalt not make me jealous. I love thee too well to suspect thee.

LADY DUNCE: Ah, but how long will you do so?

SIR DAVY: How long! As long as I live, I warrant thee, I. Don't talk to a body so. I cannot hold out if thou dost. My eyes will run over. Poor fool, poor birdie! Poor lambkin!

LADY DUNCE: But will you be so kind to me as to answer my desires? Will you make that traitor sensible that I have too just an esteem of you not to value his addresses?

SIR DAVY: Ay, ay, I will.

LADY DUNCE: But don't stay away too long, dear. I shall be in pain till I see you again.

SIR DAVY: My dear, my love, my babby, I'll be with thee in a moment. How happy am I above the rest of men! Neighbour, dear neighbour, walk in with my wife. Keep her company till I return. Child, don't be troubled, prithee don't be troubled. Was there ever such a wife? Well, da, da, da. Don't be troubled, prithee, don't be troubled, prithee, don't be troubled. Da, da.

Exit SIR DAVY and VERMIN.

LADY DUNCE: Sir Jolly, Sir Jolly, Sir Jolly!

SIR JOLLY: 'Don't be troubled, prithee don't be troubled. Da, da.'

LADY DUNCE: But, Sir Jolly, can you guess whereabout my wandering officer may be found now?

SIR JOLLY: Found, lady? He is to be at my house, lady. He's certainly one of the finest fellows in the world.

LADY DUNCE: You speak like his friend, Sir Jolly.

SIR JOLLY: His friend, lady? No, madam, his foe, his utter enemy. I shall be his ruin. I shall undo him.

LADY DUNCE: Then you may, if you please, come both and play at cards this evening with me for an hour or two, for I have contrived it that Sir David is to be abroad at supper tonight. He cannot possibly avoid it. I long to win some of the captain's money strangely.

SIR JOLLY: Do you so, my gamester? Well, I'll be sure to bring him and for what he carries about him I'll warrant you – od, he's a pretty fellow, a very pretty fellow. He has only one fault.

LADY DUNCE: And what is that, I beseech you, sir?

SIR JOLLY: Only too loving, too good-natured, that's all. 'Tis the best-natured fool breathing, that's all his fault, that's all.

SCENE THREE

BEAUGARD: (*Aside.*) What the devil shall I do to recover this day's loss? My honourable pimp too, my pander knight has forsaken me. Methinks I am like one going with a party to discover the enemy's camp but has lost his guide upon the mountains.

Enter SIR DAVY.

Curse on him. Old Argus is here again. There can be no good fortune for me when he's at my heels.

SIR DAVY: Sir, sir, sir, one word with you, sir! Captain, captain, noble captain, one word, I beseech you.

BEAUGARD: With me, friend?

SIR DAVY: Yes, with you, my no friend.

BEAUGARD: Sir David, my intimate, my bosom physician.

SIR DAVY: (*Aside.*) Ah rogue! Damned rogue!

BEAUGARD: My confessor, my dearest friend I ever had.

SIR DAVY: (*Aside.*) Dainty wheedler! Here's a fellow for ye.

BEAUGARD: One that has taught me to be in love with virtue and shown me the ugly inside of my follies.

SIR DAVY: Sir, your humble servant.

BEAUGARD: Is that all? If you are as cold in your love as you are in your friendship, Sir Davy, your lady has the worst time of't of anyone in Christendom.

SIR DAVY: So she has, sir, when she cannot be free from the insolent solicitations of such fellows as you, sir.

BEAUGARD: As me, sir? Why, who am I, good Sir Domine Doddlepate?

SIR DAVY: (*Aside.*) So, take notice he threatens me. I'll have him bound to the peace instantly. Will you never have remorse of conscience, friend? Have you banished all shame from your soul? Do you consider my name is Sir Davy Dunce? That I have the most virtuous wife living? Do you consider that? (*Aside.*) Now, how like a rogue he looks again! What a hangdog leer was that!

BEAUGARD: Your virtuous wife, sir? You are always harping upon that string, Sir Davy.

SIR DAVY: No, 'tis you would be harping upon that string, sir. See you this? Cast your eyes upon this, this letter, sir. (*SIR DAVY gives BEAUGARD the letter.*) Did not you promise this very day to abandon all manner of proceedings of this nature tending to the dishonour of me and my family?

BEAUGARD: Letter, sir? (*Aside.*) What the devil does he mean now? Let me see. (*Reads.*) 'For the Lady Dunce.' This is no scrawl of mine, I'll be sworn. By Jove, her own hand! What a dog was I! Forty to one but I had played the fool and spoiled all again. Was there ever so charming a creature breathing! (*To SIR DAVY.*) Did your lady deliver this to your hands, sir?

SIR DAVY: Even her own self in person, sir, and bade me tell you, sir, that she has too just an esteem of me, sir, not to value such a fellow as you, sir, as you deserve.

BEAUGARD: Very good. (*Reads the letter.*) 'I doubt not but this letter will surprise you.' (*Aside.*) And so it does extremely. 'But reflect upon the manner of conveying it to your hand as kindly as you can.'

SIR DAVY: Ay, you damned thief, to have it thrown into her chair by a footman!

BEAUGARD: (*Reads.*) 'Would Sir Davy were but half so kind to you as I am.'

SIR DAVY: Write you so to her, you insinuating knave?

BEAUGARD: (*Reads.*) 'But he, I am satisfied, is so severely jealous that unless you contrive some way to let me see you this evening I fear all will be hopeless.'

SIR DAVY: Impudent traitor! I might have been a monster before I'd got my supper in my belly.

BEAUGARD: (*Reads.*) 'Therefore I beseech you to appear half an hour hence in the Piazza where more may be considered of. Adieu.'

SIR DAVY: You are come, I see, accordingly. But, as a friend, I am bound in conscience to tell you the trick won't pass. You may put up your pipes and march off. (*Aside.*) O Lord! He lie with my wife! Pugh-h-h! He make Sir Davy Dunce a cuckold! Poor wretch! Ha, ha, ha!

Enter SIR JOLLY JUMBLE.

SIR JOLLY: (*Aside, to BEAUGARD.*) Hist, hist, hist.

Enter LADY DUNCE and FOURBIN disguised.

LADY DUNCE: (*To FOURBIN.*) That's he, there he is! Succeed and be rewarded.

FOURBIN: (*Aside.*) Other people may think what they please but, in my own opinion, I am a very pretty fellow. If my design succeed upon this old baboon, I'll be canonised.

SIR JOLLY: (*Aside.*) Beaugard, Beaugard! Hist, hist! Here, here! Quickly! Hist!

Exeunt BEAUGARD and SIR JOLLY JUMBLE.

FOURBIN: (*To SIR DAVY.*) Sir, sir, sir.

SIR DAVY: Friend, with me? Would you speak with me, friend?

FOURBIN: Sir, my commands are to attend your worship.

SIR DAVY: Where do you live, sweetheart, and who do you belong to?

FOURBIN: Sir, I am a small instrument of the city. I serve the Lord Mayor in his office there.

SIR DAVY: How! The Lord Mayor!

FOURBIN: Yes, sir, who desires you by all means to do him the honour of your company at supper this evening.

SIR DAVY: It will be the greatest honour I ever received in my life. What, my Lord Mayor invite me to supper? I am his lordship's most humble servant.

FOURBIN: He desires you moreover to make what haste you can, for he has matters of importance to communicate to your honour which may take up some time.

LADY DUNCE: (*Aside.*) I hope it will succeed.

SIR DAVY: Communicate with me! He does me too noble a favour. I'll fly upon the wings of ambition to lay myself at his footstool. (*Aside.*) My Lord Mayor sends himself to invite me to supper – to communicate with me too! I shall be a great man.

FOURBIN: What answer will your worship charge me back withal?

SIR DAVY: Let his lordship know that I am amazed and confounded at his generosity and that I am so transported with the honour he does me that I will not fail to wait on him in the roasting of an egg.

FOURBIN: I am your worship's lowly slave.

Exit FOURBIN.

SCENE FOUR

SIR DAVY: Vermin, go get the coach ready. Get me the gold medal too and chain which I took from the Roman Catholic officer for a popish relic.

Exit VERMIN.

I'll be fine. I'll shine and drink wine that's divine. My Lord Mayor invite me to supper!

LADY DUNCE: My dearest, I'm glad to see thee returned in safety from the bottom of my heart. Hast thou seen the traitor?

SIR DAVY: Seen him? Hang him, I have seen him. Pox on him! Seen him!

LADY DUNCE: Well, and what is become of him? Where is he?

SIR DAVY: What a pox care I what becomes of him? Prithee don't trouble me with thy impertinence. I am busy.

LADY DUNCE: You are not angry, my dear, are you?

SIR DAVY: No. I am pleased, very much pleased, let me tell you. I am to sup with my Lord Mayor, that's all, nothing else in the world. Only the business of the nation calls upon me, that's all. Therefore once more I say don't be troublesome but stand off.

LADY DUNCE: You always think my company troublesome. You never stay at home to comfort me. What think you I shall do alone by myself all this evening, moping in my chamber? Pray, my joy, stay with me for once. (*Aside.*) I hope he won't take me at my word.

SIR DAVY: I say again and again, tempter, stand off. I will not lose my preferment for my pleasure. Honour is come upon me and flesh and blood are my aversion.

LADY DUNCE: But how long will you stay?

SIR DAVY: I don't know. Maybe an hour, maybe all night as his lordship and I think fit. What's that to anybody?

LADY DUNCE: You are very cruel to me.

SIR DAVY: I can't help it. Go, pass away the time with your neighbour. I'll be back before I die. In the meantime be humble and conformable. Go.

Enter VERMIN.

Is the coach ready?

VERMIN: Yes, sir.

SIR DAVY: (*To LADY DUNCE.*) Well, your servant. What? Nothing to my Lady Mayoress? You have a great deal of breeding indeed, a great deal. Nothing to my Lady Mayoress?

LADY DUNCE: (*Weeping.*) My service to her, if you please.

SIR DAVY: Well, da, da. The poor fool cries, o' my conscience! Adieu. Do you hear? Farewell.

Exeunt SIR DAVY and VERMIN.

LADY DUNCE: As well as what I love can make me.

Enter SIR JOLLY.

SIR JOLLY: Is he gone?

LADY DUNCE: In post-haste.

SIR JOLLY: Joy go with him.

LADY DUNCE: Do you, Sir Jolly, conduct the captain hither while I dispose of the household, that he and I may be private.

SCENE FIVE

SIR DAVY's house

Enter SIR DAVY.

SIR DAVY: Troth, I had forgot my medal and chain, quite and clean forgot my relic. I was forced to come up these back stairs for fear of meeting my wife again. It is the troublesom'st loving fool. I would not have her catch me for a guinea.

Exit SIR DAVY. Enter SIR DAVY.

I must into my closet and write a short letter too. 'Tis postnight, I had forgot that.

Exit SIR DAVY.

Enter BEAUGARD and LADY DUNCE.

BEAUGARD: Are you very certain, madam, nobody is this way? I fancy as I entered I saw the glimpse of something more than ordinary.

LADY DUNCE: Is it your care of me or your personal fears that make you so suspicious? Whereabouts was the apparition?

BEAUGARD: There, there, just at that very door.

LADY DUNCE: Fie for shame! That's Sir Davy's chamber and he, I am satisfied, is far enough off by this time. I'm sure I heard the coach drive him away. But to convince you you shall see now. (*Knocking at the closet-door.*) Sir Davy, Sir Davy, Sir Davy! Look you there. You a captain and afraid of a shadow. Come, sir, shall we call for the cards?

BEAUGARD: And what shall we play for, pretty one?

LADY DUNCE: What you think best, sir.

BEAUGARD: Silver kisses or golden joys? Come, let us lay stakes a little.

Enter SIR JOLLY JUMBLE, unobserved by BEAUGARD and LADY DUNCE.

SIR JOLLY: (*Aside.*) Ah rogue, ah rogue! Are you there? Have I caught you in faith? Now, now, now!

LADY DUNCE: And who shall keep them?

BEAUGARD: You, till Sir Davy returns from supper.

LADY DUNCE: That may be long enough for our engine, Fourbin, has orders not to give him over suddenly.

BEAUGARD: And is't to yourself I'm obliged for this blessed opportunity? Let us improve it to love's best advantage.

SIR JOLLY: (*Aside.*) Ah-h-h-h! Ah-h-h-h!

BEAUGARD: Let's vow eternal [love] and raise our thoughts to expectation of immortal pleasures. In one another's eyes let's read our joys till we've no longer power o'er our desires, drunk with this dissolving – oh!

Enter SIR DAVY from his chamber.

LADY DUNCE: (*Squeaks.*) Ah!

BEAUGARD: By this light, the cuckold! Presto! Nay then, halloo!

BEAUGARD gets up and runs away.

SIR DAVY: O Lord, a man! A man in my wife's chamber! Murder, murder! Thieves, thieves! Shut up my doors! Madam! Madam! Madam!

SIR JOLLY: (*Coming forward.*) Ay, ay, thieves, thieves! Murder, murder! Where, neighbour, where, where?

LADY DUNCE catches up BEAUGARD's sword which he had left behind him in the hurry and presents it to SIR DAVY.

LADY DUNCE: Pierce this wretched heart hard to the hilts. Dye this in deepest crimson of my blood. Spare not a miserable woman's life whom heaven designed to be the unhappy object of the most horrid usage man e'er acted.

SIR DAVY: What in the name of Satan does she mean now?

LADY DUNCE: Curse on my fatal beauty! Blasted ever be these two baneful eyes that could inspire a barbarous villain to attempt such crimes as all my blood's too little to atone for! Nay, you shall hear me.

SIR DAVY: Hear you, madam? No, I have seen too much, I thank you heartily. Hear you?

LADY DUNCE: Yes and before I die I'll be justified.

SIR DAVY: Justified! O Lord, justified!

LADY DUNCE: Notice being given me of your return, I came with speed to this unhappy place where I have oft been blessed with your embraces when from behind the arras out starts Beaugard. How he came there, heaven knows.

SIR DAVY: I'll have him hanged for burglary. He has broken my house and broke the peace upon my wife. Very good!

LADY DUNCE: Straight in his arms he grasped me fast. With much ado I plunged and got my freedom, ran to your chamber door, knocked and implored your aid but all in vain.

SIR DAVY: Ha!

LADY DUNCE: Again he seized me, stopped my mouth and with a conqueror's fury –

SIR DAVY: O Lord! O Lord! No more, no more, I beseech thee. I shall grow mad and very mad. I'll plough up rocks and iron bars. I'll crack the frame of nature, sally out like Tamburlaine upon the Trojan Horse and drive the pygmies all like geese before me. O Lord, stop her mouth? Well? And how? And what then? Stopped thy mouth! Well! Ha!

LADY DUNCE: No, though unfortunate I still am innocent. His cursed purpose could not be accomplished. But who will live so injured? I'll die to be revenged on myself. I ne'er can hope to see his streaming gore so thus I let out my own.

LADY DUNCE offers to run upon the sword.

SIR DAVY: (*Preventing her.*) Ha! What wouldst thou do, my love? Prithee don't break my heart. If thou wilt kill, kill me. I know thou art innocent. I see thou art. I had rather be a cuckold a thousand times than lose thee, poor love, poor dearee, poor baby.

SIR JOLLY: (*Weeps.*) Alack-a-day!

LADY DUNCE: (*Sinking to her knees.*) Ah me!

SIR DAVY: Ah, prithee be comforted now. Why, I'll love thee the better for this. Why shouldst thou be troubled for another's ill doings? I know it was no fault of thine.

SIR JOLLY: No, no more it was not, I swear.

SIR DAVY: See, see, my neighbour weeps too. He's troubled to see thee thus.

LADY DUNCE: O, but revenge!

SIR DAVY: Why, thou shalt have revenge. I'll have him murdered. I'll have his throat cut before tomorrow morning, child. Rise now, prithee rise.

SIR JOLLY: Ay, do, madam, and smile upon Sir Davy.

LADY DUNCE: But will you love me then as well as e'er you did?

SIR DAVY: Ay, and the longest day I live too.

LADY DUNCE: And shall I have justice done me on that prodigious monster?

SIR DAVY: Why, he shall be crows' meat by tomorrow night. I tell thee he shall be crows' meat by midnight, chicken.

LADY DUNCE: (*Rising.*)
Then I will live since 'tis something so pleasant
When I in peace may lead a happy life
With such a husband.

SIR DAVY: I with such a wife.

ACT FOUR

SCENE ONE

The tavern.

Enter BEAUGARD, COURTINE and DRAWER.

DRAWER: Welcome, gentlemen, very welcome, sir. Will you please to walk up one pair of stairs?

BEAUGARD: Get the great room ready. Carry up a good stock of bottles with ice to cool our wine and water to refresh our glasses.

DRAWER: It shall be done, sir.

CUSTOMERS call offstage.

Coming, coming there, coming. (*To SERVANTS offstage.*) Speak up in the Dolphin, somebody!

Exit DRAWER.

BEAUGARD: Ah, Courtine, must we be always idle? Must we never see our glorious days again? When shall we be rolling in the lands of milk and honey, encamped in large, luxuriant vineyards where loaded vines cluster about our tents, drink the rich juice just pressed from the plump grape, feeding on all the fragrant fruit that grow in fertile climes, ripened by the vigour of the sun?

COURTINE: Ah, Beaugard, those days have been.

BEAUGARD: Ay, now we are home in our hives and sleep like drones.

COURTINE: Now we must content ourselves at a humble rate.

BEAUGARD: Prithee, no more hints of poverty, Ned. 'Tis scandalous. 'Sdeath, dost thou want money?

COURTINE: True, I want no necessaries to keep me alive but I do not enjoy myself. I would have it in my power, when he needed me, to serve and assist my friend. I would deal handsomely too with the woman that pleased me.

BEAUGARD: O, fie for shame! You would be a whoremaster. Friend, go, go. I'll have no more to do with you.

COURTINE: It turns my stomach to wheedle with a rogue I scorn who uses me scurvily because he has my name in his shop book.

BEAUGARD: Or to use respects and ceremonies to the milch cow his wife and praise his pretty brats though they stink of their mother and are uglier than the issue of a baboon. Yet all this must be endured.

COURTINE: Must it, Beaugard?

BEAUGARD: And since 'tis so, let's think of a bottle.

COURTINE: With all my heart, for railing and drinking do much better together than by themselves. A private room, a trusty friend, good wine and bold truths are my happiness. But where's our friend and intimate, Sir Jolly, this evening?

BEAUGARD: I parted with him just now. He's gone to contrive me a meeting, if possible this night, with the woman my soul is fond of. I was this evening just entering upon the palace of all joy when that plague to all well meaning women, the husband, came unseasonably by and forced a poor lover to his heels that was fairly making his progress another way.

COURTINE: Why didst thou not murder the saucy, intruding clown? To dare to disturb a gentleman's privacies! I would have beaten him into good sense of his transgression,

enjoyed his wife before his face and taught the dog his
duty.

BEAUGARD: Do you think, Ned, you are dealing with the
landlord of your winter quarters in Alsatia?

COURTINE: O, you are in the right! There has to be a
difference observed between your arbitrary whoring and
your limited fornication.

BEAUGARD: Though we may make bold with another man's
wife in a friendly way, yet nothing by compulsion, dear
heart.

COURTINE: And now Sir Jolly, I hope, is to be the instrument
of some new immortal plot.

BEAUGARD: Sir Jolly! Why, on my conscience, he believes it
his undoubted right to be pimp master-general to London
and Middlesex. Nay, he keeps a catalogue of the choicest
beauties about town illustrated with an account of their
age, shape, proportion, colour of hair and eyes, degrees of
complexion, gunpowder-spots, moles...

COURTINE: I wish the old pander would satisfy my curiosity
as to what marks of nature my Sylvia has about her.

Enter SIR JOLLY JUMBLE.

SIR JOLLY: My captains! My sons of Mars, my imps of Venus!
Well encountered! What, shall we have a sparkling bottle
or two and use fortune like a jade? Beaugard, you are a
rogue, you are a dog. I hate you. Get you gone, go.

BEAUGARD: Sir Jolly, what news from paradise? Is there any
hope I shall come there tonight?

SIR JOLLY: Maybe there is, maybe there is not. I say let us
have a bottle. I will say nothing else without a bottle. After
a glass or two my heart may open.

COURTINE: Why then, we will have a bottle, Sir Jolly.

SIR JOLLY: Will? We'll have dozens and drink till we're wise and speak well of nobody, till we are lewder than midnight-whores and outrail disbanded officers.

BEAUGARD: Only one thing more, my noble knight, and then we are entirely at thy disposal.

SIR JOLLY: Well, and what's that? What's the business?

BEAUGARD: This friend of mine here stands in need of thy assistance. He's damnably in love, Sir Jolly.

SIR JOLLY: In love! Is he so? In love! Od's my life! What's her name? Where does she live? I warrant you I know her. She's in my table-book, I warrant you. (*Pulls out a table-book.*) Virgin, wife or widow?

COURTINE: In troth, Sir Jolly, that's a difficult question but as virgins go she may pass for one of them.

SIR JOLLY: Virgin. Very good. Let me see. Virgin, virgin, virgin. Oh here are the virgins. Truly, I meet with the fewest of this sort of any. Well, and the first letter of her name now? For a wager, I'll guess her.

COURTINE: Then know, Sir Jolly, that I love my love with an S.

SIR JOLLY: S. S. S. Oh here are the Esses. Let me consider now. Sappho?

COURTINE: No, sir.

SIR JOLLY: Selinda?

COURTINE: Neither.

SIR JOLLY: Sophronia?

COURTINE: Guess again.

SIR JOLLY: Sylvia?

COURTINE: Ay, Sir Jolly, that's the fatal name. Sylvia, the fair, the witty, the ill-natured. Do you know her, my friend?

SIR JOLLY: Know her? Why, she is my daughter. I adopted her these seven years. Sylvia – let me look. (*Reads.*) 'Light brown hair, her face oval and Roman, quick sparkling eyes, plump, pregnant, ruby lips with a mole on her breast and the perfect likeness of a heart-cherry on her left knee.' Ah villain! Ah sly-cap! Have I caught you? Are you there, i'faith? Well, and what says she? Is she coming? Do her eyes betray her? Does her heart beat and her bubbies rise when you talk to her, ha?

BEAUGARD: Look you, Sir Jolly, all things considered, it may come to a marriage in time.

SIR JOLLY: I'll have nothing to do with it. I won't be seen in the business of matrimony. Make me a matchmaker, a filthy marriage broker? Sir, I scorn. I know better things. Look you, friend, to carry her a letter from you, though it be in a church I'll deliver it. Or, when the business is come to an issue, if I may bring you handsomely together, and so forth, I'll serve thee with all my soul and thank thee heartily, dear rogue. I will, you little cock sparrow, faith and troth, I will. But no matrimony. I'll have nothing to do with matrimony. 'Tis a damned invention and a destroyer of civil correspondence.

Enter DRAWER.

DRAWER: Gentlemen, your room is ready, your wine and ice upon the table. Will your honours please to walk in?

SIR JOLLY: Ay, wine, wine, give us wine. A pox on matrimony! Matrimony, in the devil's name!

COURTINE: (*To DRAWER.*) But if an honest harlot or two inquire for us –

SIR JOLLY: Right, sirrah, if whores come never so many, give 'em reverence and reception. But nothing else! Let nothing but whores and bottles come near us, as you value your ears.

They go within the scene, where is discovered table and bottles.

BEAUGARD: Why, there's the land of Canaan now in little. Hark you, Drawer, dog, shut the door – do you hear? – shut it so close that neither care nor necessity peep in on us.

The scene closes upon BEAUGARD and COURTINE.

Enter FOURBIN and BLOODY BONES.

FOURBIN: (*Aside.*) Bloody Bones, my lady says we must be expeditious. Behave yourself handsomely. Show yourself a cut-throat and nothing is wanting to keep the whore Fortune under.

Enter SIR DAVY.

DRAWER: Welcome, gentlemen, very welcome, sir. Will't please you to walk into a room? Or shall I wait upon your honours' pleasure here?

SIR DAVY: Sweetheart, let us be private and bring us wine hither.

Exit DRAWER. He returns with wine and glasses then exits again.

So. (*Sits.*) From this moment, war! War and mortal dudgeon against that enemy of my honour and thief of my good name called Beaugard. (*To FOURBIN.*) You can cut a throat upon occasion, you say, friend?

FOURBIN: Sir, cutting of throats is my hereditary vocation. My father was hanged for cutting of throats before me and my mother for cutting of purses.

SIR DAVY: No more to be said. My courage is mounted like a little Frenchman upon a great horse. I'll have him murdered.

FOURBIN: Sir, 'murdered' you say, sir?

SIR DAVY: Ay, 'murdered' I say, sir. His face flayed off and nailed to a post in my great hall in the country amongst all the other trophies of wild beasts slain by our family since the Conquest.

FOURBIN: Sir, for that let me recommend this worthy friend of mine. He's an industrious gentleman and one that will deserve your favour.

SIR DAVY: He looks but ruggedly though, methinks.

FOURBIN: Sir, his parts will atone for his person. He affects a sort of philosophical negligence but make trial of him and you'll find him a person fit for the work of this world.

SIR DAVY: What trade are you, friend?

BLOODY BONES: No trade at all, friend. Rascally butchers make a trade of't. To a gentleman, 'tis a divertisement.

SIR DAVY: Do you profess murder?

BLOODY BONES: Yes, sir, 'tis my livelihood. I keep a wife and six children by it.

SIR DAVY: (*Drinks to him.*) Then, sir, here's to you with all my heart. (*Aside.*) Would I had done with these fellows.

FOURBIN: Sir, if you have any service for us, I desire we may receive your gold and your instructions.

BLOODY BONES: In peaceable times a man may eat and drink comfortably upon't. A private murder done handsomely is worth money. But now that the nation's unsettled so many undertaker the profession you may have a man murdered for little or nothing and nobody e'er know who did it neither.

SIR DAVY: Pray what countryman are you, most noble sir?

BLOODY BONES: My country is foreign. I was born in Algier. My mother was an apostate Greek, my father a renegado Englishman who by oppressing Christian slaves grew rich, for which, when he lay sick, I murdered him one day in his bed, made my escape to Malta where, embracing the faith, I had given me to command a thousand horse aboard the galleys of that state.

SIR DAVY: O Lord, sir! My humble service to you again.

FOURBIN: He tells you but the naked truth.

SIR DAVY: I doubt it not in the least, most worthy sir. (*Aside.*) These are devilish fellows, I'll warrant 'em.

FOURBIN: War, friend, and shining honour has been our province till rusty peace reduced us to this base obscurity. Ah, Bloody Bones! Ah, when thou and I commanded that party at the siege of Philippsville, in the face of the army we took the impenetrable half-moon!

BLOODY BONES: Half-moon, sir! By your favour, 'twas a whole moon.

SIR DAVY: I doubt it not in the least, gentlemen, but in the meanwhile to our business.

FOURBIN: With all my heart.

SIR DAVY: Do you know this Beaugard? He's a devilish fellow, I can tell you but that. He's a captain.

FOURBIN: Has he a heart, think you, sir?

SIR DAVY: O, like a lion! He fears neither God, man nor devil.

BLOODY BONES: I'll bring it you for your breakfast tomorrow. Did you never eat a man's heart, sir?

SIR DAVY: Eat a man's heart, friend?

FOURBIN: Ay, ay, a man's heart, sir. It makes absolutely the best ragout in the world. I have eaten forty of 'em in my time without bread.

SIR DAVY: O Lord! A man's heart! My humble service to you both, gentlemen.

BLOODY BONES: Why, your Algerian pirates eat nothing else at sea. They have them potted like venison. Your Dutchman's heart makes an excellent dish with oil and pepper.

SIR DAVY: Oh Lord! Oh Lord! (*To FOURBIN.*) Friend, a word with you. How much must you and your companion have to do this business?

FOURBIN: What and bring you the heart to your house?

SIR DAVY: No, no, keeping the heart for your own eating. (*Aside.*) I'll be rid of 'em as soon as possible I can.

FOURBIN: You say, sir, he's a gentleman?

SIR DAVY: Ay, such a sort of gentleman as are about in this town. The fellow has a pretty handsome outside but, I believe, little or no money in his pockets.

FOURBIN: Therefore we are like to receive more from your worship's bounty.

BLOODY BONES: I care for no man's bounty. I expect to have my bargain performed and I'll make as good a one as I can.

SIR DAVY: Look you, friend, don't you be angry, before you have occasion. You say you'll have – let's see, how much will you have now? (*Aside.*) I warrant the devil and all, by your good will.

FOURBIN: Truly, Sir David, if, as you say, the man must be well murdered without any remorse or mercy, betwixt Turk and Jew it is honestly worth two hundred pounds.

SIR DAVY: Two hundred pounds! Why, I'll have a physician shall kill a whole family for half the money.

BLOODY BONES: Damme, sir, how do ye mean?

SIR DAVY: Damme, sir, how do I mean? Damme, sir, not to part with my money.

BLOODY BONES: Not part, brother?
Have I for this dissolved Circean charms,
Broke iron durance, whilst from these firm legs
The well-filed useless fetters dropped away
And left me master of my native freedom?

SIR DAVY: What does he mean now?

FOURBIN: Truly, sir, I am sorry to see it with all my heart. 'Tis a distraction that frequently seizes him. I am sorry it should happen so unluckily at this time.

SIR DAVY: Distracted, say you? Is he so apt to be distracted?

FOURBIN: Oh, sir, raging mad. We that live by murder are all so. Guilt will never let us sleep. I beseech you, sir, stand clear of him. He's apt to be very mischievous at these unfortunate hours.

BLOODY BONES:
Have I been drunk with tender infants' blood
And ripped up teeming wombs? Have these bold hands
Ransacked the temples of the gods and stabbed
The priests before their altars? Have I done this?
Ha!

SIR DAVY: No, sir, not that I know, sir. I would not say any such thing for all the world, sir. (*To FOURBIN.*) Worthy gentleman, I beseech you, sir, you seem to be a civil person. I beseech you, sir, to mitigate his passion. I'll do anything in the world. You shall command my whole estate.

FOURBIN: Nay, after all, sir, if you have not a mind to have him quite murdered, if a swingeing drubbing to bed-rid him or so will serve your turn, you may have it at a cheaper rate.

SIR DAVY: Truly, sir, with all my heart for methinks, now I consider matters better, I would not by any means be guilty of another man's blood.

FOURBIN: Why then, let me consider. To have him beaten substantially, a beating that will stick by him, will cost you – half the money.

SIR DAVY: What, one hundred pounds! Sure the devil's in you or you would not be so unconscionable.

BLOODY BONES:
The devil? Where? Where is the devil? Show me.
I'll tell thee, Beelzebub, thou hast broke thy covenant.
Didst thou not promise me eternal plenty
When I resigned my soul to thy allurements?

SIR DAVY: Ah, Lord!

BLOODY BONES:
Touch me not yet. I've yet ten thousand murders
To act before I'm thine. With all those sins
I'll come with full damnation to thy caverns
Of endless pain and howl with thee forever.

SIR DAVY: Bless us! What will become of this mortal body of mine? Where am I? Is this a house? Do I live? Am I flesh and blood?

BLOODY BONES:
There, there's the fiend again! Don't chatter so
And grin at me. If thou must needs have prey
Take here, take him, this tempter that would bribe me
With shining gold
To stain my hands with new iniquity.

SIR DAVY: Stand off, I charge thee, Satan, whereso'er thou art. Thou hast no right nor claim to me. I'll have thee bound in necromantic charms. (*To FOURBIN.*) Hark you, friend, has the gentleman given his soul to the devil?

FOURBIN: Only pawned it a little, that's all.

SIR DAVY: Let me beseech you, sir, to dispatch and get rid of him as soon as you can. I would gladly drink a bottle with you, sir, but I hate the devil's company mortally. As for the hundred pound, here, here it is ready. (*Gives FOURBIN money.*) No more words. I'll submit to your good nature and discretion.

FOURBIN: (*To BLOODY BONES.*) Then, wretch, take this (*Giving him money.*) and make thy peace with the infernal king. He loves riches. Sacrifice and be at rest.

BLOODY BONES: 'Tis done. I'll follow thee. Lead on. Nay, if thou smile I more defy thee. Fee, fo, fa, fum.

Exit BLOODY BONES.

FOURBIN: 'Tis very odd, this.

SIR DAVY: Very odd indeed. I'm glad he's gone though.

FOURBIN: Now, sir, if you please, we'll refresh ourselves with a cheerful glass and so *chaqu'un chez lui.* (*Aside.*) I would fain make the gull drunk to put a little mettle into him.

SIR DAVY: With all my heart, sir, but no more words of the devil, if you love me.

FOURBIN: The devil's an ass, sir, and here's a health (*Drinks.*) to all those that defy the devil.

SIR DAVY: With all my heart and all his works too.

FOURBIN: (*Pouring SIR DAVY a drink.*) Nay, sir, you must do me right, I assure you.

SIR DAVY: Not so full, not so full, that's too much of all conscience. In troth, friend, these are sad times, very sad times. But here's to you. (*He drinks.*)

FOURBIN: Pox o' the times. The times are well enough so long as a man has money in his pocket.

SIR DAVY: 'Tis true. Here I have been bargaining with you about a murder but never consider that idolatry is coming in full speed upon the nation. Pray what religion are you of, friend?

FOURBIN: What religion am I of, sir? Sir, your humble servant. (*He toasts SIR DAVY.*)

SIR DAVY: Truly, a good conscience is a great happiness. And so I'll pledge you. (*Drinks and chokes.*) Hemph, hemph! But shall the dog be murdered this night?

FOURBIN: My brother rogue is gone by this time to set on him. (*Drinks.*) Here's rest to his soul.

SIR DAVY: With all my heart. (*Drinks.*) Faith, I hate to be uncharitable.

Enter COURTINE and DRAWER.

COURTINE: Look you, 'tis very impudent not to be drunk. Shall rogues stay in taverns, sip pints and be sober when honest gentlemen are drunk by gallons? I'll have none of't.

SIR DAVY: (*Sits up in his chair.*) Oh Lord, who's there?

DRAWER: (*To COURTINE.*) I beseech your honour, our house will be utterly ruined by this means.

COURTINE: Damn your house, your wife, your children and all your family, you dog! (*To SIR DAVY.*) Sir, who are you?

SIR DAVY: Who am I, sir? What's that to you, sir? Will you tickle my foot, you rogue?

COURTINE: I'll tickle your guts, you poltroon, presently.

SIR DAVY: Tickle my guts, you madcap? I'll tickle your toby if you do.

COURTINE: What, with that circumcised band? Old fellow, I believe you're a rogue.

SIR DAVY: Sirrah, you are a whore, an errant bitch-whore. I'll use you like a whore. I'll kiss you, you jade. I'll ravish you, you buttock. I am a Justice of the Peace, sirrah, and that's worse.

COURTINE: Damn you, sir, I'd care not if you were a constable and all his watch. What, such a rogue as you send honest fellows to prison and countenance whores in your jurisdiction for bribery, you mongrel! I'll beat you, sirrah. I'll brain you. I'll murder you, you mooncalf.

COURTINE throws the chairs at SIR DAVY.

SIR DAVY: Sir, sir, sir! Constable! Watch! Murder!

Exit SIR DAVY.

COURTINE: Huzza, Beaugard!

Enter BEAUGARD, SIR JOLLY JUMBLE.

FOURBIN: Well, sir, the business is done. We have bargained to murder you.

BEAUGARD: Murder? Who's to be murdered? Ha, Fourbin?

SIR JOLLY: You are to be murdered, friend.

BEAUGARD: Who's to murder me, I beseech you?

FOURBIN: Your humble servant, Fourbin, with your leave. I am the man. Sir David has given me this gold to do it.

BEAUGARD: Sir David? Uncharitable cur! What, murder an honest fellow for being civil to his family?

SIR JOLLY: No, 'tis so you may be civil to his family. You are to be murdered tonight and buried abed with my lady, you rascal, you.

BEAUGARD: I understand you, gentlemen, ha!

Exit COURTINE.

FOURBIN: Your honour has a piercing judgment. Sir, Captain Courtine's gone.

BEAUGARD: Let him go. He has a design to put in practice this night too that might perhaps spoil ours. But when, Sir Jolly, is this business to be?

SIR JOLLY: At once. Go, get you gone, I say. Hold, hold, let's see your left ear first. Hum. Ha! You are a rogue. Get you gone, get you gone, go.

SCENE TWO

Covent Garden Piazza, outside SIR DAVY's house.

Enter SYLVIA and VERMIN in the balcony.

VERMIN: But, madam. why will you use him so inhumanly? I'm confident he loves you.

SYLVIA: Oh, a true lover is to be found out like a true saint, by the trial of his patience. Have you the cords ready?

VERMIN: Here they are, madam.

SYLVIA: Let 'em down. Be sure when it comes to trial to pull lustily.

They let the cords down from the balcony. Exit LADY DUNCE.

Is Will the footman ready?

FOOTMAN: (*Offstage.*) At your command, madam.

SYLVIA: Be sure when it comes to trial to pull lustily. I wonder he should stay so long. The clock has struck twelve.

Enter COURTINE below.

COURTINE: (*Sings.*) And was she not frank and free
And was she not kind to me
To lock up her cat in her cupboard
And give her key to me, to me,
To lock up her cat in her cupboard
And give her key to me?

SYLVIA: This must be he. Ay, 'tis he and, as I am a virgin, roaring drunk. But if I find not a way to make him sober –

COURTINE: Here's the window. Ay, that's hell-door and my damnation's inside. (*Calls.*) Sylvia, Sylvia, Sylvia! Dear imp of Satan, appear to thy servant.

SYLVIA: Who calls on Sylvia in this dead of night
When rest is wanting to her longing eyes?

COURTINE: 'Tis a poor wretch can hardly stand upright
Drunk with thy love and if he falls he lies.

SYLVIA: Courtine, is't you?

COURTINE: Yes, sweetheart, 'tis I. Art thou ready for me?

SYLVIA: Fasten yourself to that cord there. There, there it is.

COURTINE: Cord? Where? O, O, here, here. (*Fastens himself.*)
    So, now to heaven in a string.

SYLVIA: Have you done?

COURTINE: Yes, I have done, child, and would fain be doing
    too, hussy.

SYLVIA: (*To the SERVANTS.*) Then pull away. Hoa up, hoa up,
    hoa up.

   COURTINE is pulled halfway up to the balcony.

   So, avast there. (*To COURTINE.*) Sir.

COURTINE: Madam?

SYLVIA: Are you very much in love, sir?

COURTINE: O, damnably, child, damnably.

SYLVIA: I'm sorry for't with all my heart. Good night, captain.

   Exit SYLVIA.

COURTINE: Ha, gone! What, left between heaven and hell? If
    the constable should take me now for a straggling monkey
    hung by the loins and hunt me with his watchmen! Ah
    woman, woman, woman! Well, a merry life and a short,
    that's all.

   (*Sings.*) God prosper long our noble king,
    Our lives and safeties all.
    I am mighty loyal tonight.

   *The scene opens to show SIR DAVY's house and discovers SIR
   JOLLY JUMBLE and LADY DUNCE putting BEAUGARD in order
   as if he were dead. VERMIN, FOURBIN and BLOODY BONES
   observe.*

SIR JOLLY: Lie still, lie still, you knave. You'll spoil the sport! Close, close, when I bid you.

BEAUGARD: But pray how long must I lie thus?

LADY DUNCE: I warrant you, you'll think the time mighty tedious.

BEAUGARD: Sweet creature, who can counterfeit death when you are near him?

SIR JOLLY: You shall, sirrah, if a body desires you a little, so you shall. All will be spoiled else, man. Stretch out longer, longer yet, as long as ever you can. So, so. Hold your breath, hold your breath. Very well.

LADY DUNCE: Here comes Sir David.

FOURBIN and BLOODY BONES go out from SIR DAVY's house.

FOURBIN: Murder, murder, murder! Help, help, murder!

COURTINE: Nay, if there be murder stirring, 'tis high time to shift myself.

COURTINE climbs up to the balcony.

BLOODY BONES: Murder! Murder! Murder!

SIR JOLLY: (*To BEAUGRAD.*) Od's so, now close again as I told you. Close, you devil! Now stir if you dare. Stir any part about you if you dare now. Od, I'll hit you such a rap if you do. Lie still, lie you still.

SYLVIA: (*Offstage, squeaking.*) Ah-h-h-h!

BLOODY BONES: Yonder, yonder he comes.

Enter SIR DAVY.

FOURBIN / BLOODY BONES: Murder, murder, murder!

SIR DAVY: 'Tis very late but murder is a melancholy business and night is fit for't. I'll go home.

He knocks at his house door.

VERMIN: (*Inside.*) Who's there?

SIR DAVY: 'Who's there?' Open the door, you whelp of
Babylon.

VERMIN: (*Opening the door.*) O sir, you're welcome home
but here is the saddest news! Here has been murder
committed, sir.

SIR DAVY: Hold your tongue, you fool, and go to sleep. Get
you in, do you hear? You talk of murder, you rogue? You
meddle with state-affairs? Get you in.

He goes in.

My dear, how dost thou do, my dear? I am come.

LADY DUNCE: Ah sir! What is't you've done? You've ruined
me, your family, your fortune. All is ruined. Where shall
we go? Whither shall we fly?

SIR DAVY: 'Where shall we go?' Why, we'll go to bed, you
little jackadandy. Why, you are not a wench, you rogue,
you are a boy, a very boy and I love you the better for't,
sirrah, hey!

LADY DUNCE: Ah sir, see there.

SIR DAVY: Bless us, a man! And bloody! What, upon my hall
table!

LADY DUNCE: Two ruffians brought him in just now,
pronouncing the inhuman deed was done by your
command. Sir Jolly came in that minute or sure I had
died with my distracting fears. How could you think of a
revenge so horrid?

SIR DAVY: As I hope to be saved, neighbour, I only bargained
with 'em to bastinado him in a way or so as one friend
might do another. But do you say that he is dead?

SIR JOLLY: Dead, dead as clay, stark stiff and useless all. Nothing about him stirring but all's cold and still. I knew him a lusty fellow once, a very mettled fellow. 'Tis a thousand pities.

SIR DAVY: What shall I do? I'll throw myself upon him, kiss his wide wounds and weep till I'm blind as a buzzard.

LADY DUNCE: O come not near him. There's such horrid antipathy follows all murders, his wounds would stream afresh should you but touch him.

SIR DAVY: Dear neighbour, dearest neighbour, friend, Sir Jolly, as you love charity, pity my wretched case and give me counsel. I'll give my wife and all my estate to have him live again. Or shall I bury him in the arbour at the upper end of the garden?

SIR JOLLY: Alas-a-day, neighbour, never think of't. The dogs will find him there as they scrape holes to bury bones. There is but one way that I know of.

SIR DAVY: (*Kneeling.*) What is it, dear neighbour? What is it? You see I am upon my knees to you. Take all I have and ease me of my fears.

SIR JOLLY: Truly, the best thing I can think of is putting him into a warm bed and try to fetch him to life again. A warm bed is the best thing in the world. My lady may do much too. She's a good woman and, as I've been told, understands a green wound well.

SIR DAVY: My dear, my dear, my dear!

LADY DUNCE: Bear me away. Oh send me hence far off where my unhappy name may be a stranger and this sad accident no more remembered to my dishonour.

SIR DAVY: Ah, but, my love, my joy, are there no bowels in thee?

LADY DUNCE: What would you have me do?

SIR DAVY: Prithee try thy skill. There may be one dram of life left in him yet. Take him to thy chamber, put him into thy bed and try what thou canst do with him. Prithee do. If thou canst but find motion in him, all may yet be well. I'll go up to my closet in the garret and say my prayers.

LADY DUNCE: Will ye then leave this ruin on my hands?

SIR DAVY: Pray, pray, my dear. (*To SIR JOLLY.*) I beseech you, neighbour, help persuade her if it be possible.

SIR JOLLY: Faith, madam, try what you can do. I have a great fancy you may do him good. Who can tell but you may have the gift of stroking? Pray, be persuaded.

LADY DUNCE: I'll do whate'er's your pleasure.

SIR DAVY: That's my best dear. I'll go to my chamber and pray for thee heartily. Alas, alas, that ever this should happen!

Exit SIR DAVY.

BEAUGARD: So, is he gone, madam, my angel?

SIR JOLLY: What, no thanks, no reward for old Jolly now? Come hither, hussy, you little canary-bird, you little hop-o'-my-thumb, come hither. Make me a curtsy and give me a kiss now. Ha! Give me a kiss, I say. Od, I will have a kiss, so I will, I will have a kiss if I set on't. (*They kiss.*) Shoo, shoo, shoo! Get you into a corner when I bid you. Shoo, shoo, shoo!

LADY DUNCE goes to BEAUGARD.

What, there already? Well, I ha' done, I ha' done. This 'tis to be an old fellow.

BEAUGARD: And will you save the life of him you've wounded?

LADY DUNCE: Dare you trust yourself to my skill for a cure?

SIR DAVY appears at a window above.

SIR JOLLY: Hist, hist! Close, close, I say again! Yonder's Sir Davy. Od's so!

SIR DAVY: My dear, my dear! My dear!

LADY DUNCE: Who's that calls? My love, is't you?

SIR DAVY: Ah, some comfort or my heart's broke. I've tried to say my prayers and cannot. If he be quite dead, I shall never pray again. Neighbour, no hopes?

SIR JOLLY: Truly little or none. Some small pulse there is left, very little. There's nothing to be done if you don't pray. Get you to prayers. Get you gone. Nay, don't stay now. Shut the window, I tell you.

SIR DAVY: Well, this is a great trouble to me. But good-night.

SIR JOLLY: Good-night to you, dear neighbour.

Exit SIR DAVY.

(*To BEAUGARD and LADY DUNCE.*) Get ye up and be gone into the next room. Make haste. But don't stir till I come to you. Be sure ye remember, to Sir Davy's lodgings that he may be safe and be with you in a twinkle. Ah-h-h-h!

Exeunt BEAUGARD and LADY DUNCE.

So, now for the door. (*Bolts the door.*) Very well, friend, you are fast.

(*Sings.*) Bonny lass, gin thou wert mine,
And twonty thoosand poonds aboot thee. (*Etc.*)

ACT FIVE

SCENE ONE

SYLVIA's chamber.

COURTINE bound on a couch.

COURTINE: (*Waking up.*) Hey ho! Ha! Where am I? Was I
drunk or no? Something leaning that way. But where the
devil am I? In a bawdy house. Faugh! What a smell of sin
is here! Let me look about. What's the matter now? Tied
fast! Bound too! What tricks have I played to come into
this condition! I have lighted into the territories of some
merrily-disposed chambermaid and she in a witty fit hath
trussed me thus. Has she pinned no rags to my tail or
chalked me upon the back? Would I had her mistress here.

SYLVIA: What would you do with her, my enchanted knight, if
you had her? You are too sober for her by this time. Next
time you get drunk, you may venture to scale her balcony,
like the valiant captain you are.

COURTINE: Hast thou done this, my dear destruction? I must
confess, when I am in my beer my courage runs away with
me. What, tie me up like an ungovernable cur? Fie upon't!
Let thy poor dog loose that he may fawn and make much
of thee.

SYLVIA: What, with those paws you have been ferreting in
Moorfields with and are very dirty still? After you have
daggled yourself abroad for prey and met with none, you
come sneaking hither for a crust, do you?

COURTINE: Indeed, indeed! But let me loose and thou shalt
see what a gentle, humble animal thou hast made me.

SYLVIA: If you should be taken into favour, would you be for rambling again so soon as you had your liberty?

COURTINE: Try me and if ever I prove recreant more, let me be beaten and used like a dog in good earnest.

SYLVIA: Promise to grant me one request and it shall be done.

COURTINE: Hear me swear.

SYLVIA: That anybody may do ten thousand times a day.

COURTINE: Upon the word of a gentleman. Nay, as I hope to get money in my pocket.

SYLVIA: There I believe him. You'll keep your word, you say?

COURTINE: If I don't, hang me up in a wench's old garters.

SYLVIA: (*Untying him.*) See, sir, you have your freedom.

COURTINE: Well, now name the price. What must I pay for't?

SYLVIA: You know, sir, considering our small acquaintance, you have been pleased to talk to me very freely of love matters.

COURTINE: I must confess I have been something to blame that way but, after this night's adventure, I swear if ever thou hear'st more of it from my mouth –

SYLVIA: Have a care of swearing, for you must understand that, spite of my teeth, I am at last fallen in love most unmercifully.

COURTINE: And dost thou imagine I am so hard-hearted a villain as to have no compassion for thee?

SYLVIA: No, for I hope he's a man you can have no exceptions against.

COURTINE: Yes, yes, the man is a man, I assure you. That's one comfort.

SYLVIA: Who do you think it may be now? Try if you can guess him.

COURTINE: Whoever he is, he's an honest fellow, I warrant him, and I believe he will not think himself very unhappy neither.

SYLVIA: If a fortune of five thousand pounds, pleasant nights and quiet days can make him happy, he may be so. But try to guess at him.

COURTINE: But if I should be mistaken?

SYLVIA: Why, who is it you would wish me to?

COURTINE: You have five thousand pounds, you say?

SYLVIA: Yes.

COURTINE: Faith, child, to deal honestly, I know well enough who 'tis I wish for. But, sweetheart, before I tell you my inclinations, it were but reasonable that I knew yours.

SYLVIA: Well, sir, I'll make a discovery. And, to hold you in suspense no longer, you must know I have a month's mind to an armful of your dearly beloved friend and brother captain Beaugard. What say you to't?

COURTINE: Madam, your humble servant, good-bye, that's all.

SYLVIA: What, thus cruelly leave a lady that so kindly took you, in your last night's pickle, into her lodging? Whither would you rove now, my wanderer?

COURTINE: Faith, madam, you have dealt so gallantly in trusting me with your passion, I cannot stay here without telling you that I am three times as much in love with an acquaintance of yours as you can be with any friend of mine.

SYLVIA: Not with my waiting-woman, I hope, sir.

COURTINE: No, but with a certain kinswoman of thine, child. They call her my Lady Dunce and I think this is her house too. They say she will be civil upon a good occasion. Therefore be charitable and show me the way to her chamber.

SYLVIA: What, commit adultery, captain? Fie upon't! What, hazard your soul?

COURTINE: No, no, only venture my body a little, that's all. Look you, now you know my secret and may imagine my desires. Therefore, as you would have me assist your inclinations, pray be civil and help me to mine. No demurring upon the matter, no qualms but show me the way for I will go.

SYLVIA: But you shan't go, sir.

COURTINE: 'Shan't go', lady?

SYLVIA: No, shan't go, sir. Did I not tell you when once you had got your liberty that you would be rambling again?

COURTINE: Why, child, wouldst thou be so uncharitable as to tie a poor jade to an empty rack in thy stable when he knows where to go elsewhere to get provender?

SYLVIA: Any musty provender, I find, will serve your turn so you have it cheap or at another man's charges.

COURTINE: No, child, I had rather my ox should graze in a field of my own than live hidebound upon the common or run the hazard of being impounded every day for trespass.

SYLVIA: Truly, all things considered, 'tis great pity so good a husbandman as you should want a farm to cultivate.

COURTINE: Wouldst thou be but kind as to let me have a tenement of thine to try how it would agree with me?

SYLVIA: And would you be content to take a lease for life?

COURTINE: So there is so pretty a lady of the manor and a moderate rent.

SYLVIA: Which you'll be sure to pay very punctually.

COURTINE: If thou doubt'st my honesty, faith take a little earnest beforehand.

COURTINE offers to kiss her.

SYLVIA: Not so hasty, good tenant. First: you shall oblige yourself to a constant residence and not, by leaving the house uninhabited, let it run to repairs.

COURTINE: Agreed.

SYLVIA: Second: for your own sake you shall promise to keep the estate well-fenced and enclosed lest sometime or other your neighbour's cattle break in and spoil the crop on the ground.

COURTINE: Very just and reasonable, provided I don't find it lie too much to common already.

SYLVIA: Third: you shall enter into strict covenant not to take any other farm upon your hands without my consent or if you do that then it shall be lawful for me to get me another tenant how and where I think fit.

COURTINE: Faith, that's hard, let me tell you that, landlady.

SYLVIA: Upon these terms we'll draw articles.

COURTINE: And when shall we sign 'em?

SYLVIA: Why, this morning, as soon as the ten o' clock office in Covent Garden is open.

COURTINE: A bargain. But how will you answer your entertainment of a drunken redcoat in your lodgings at this unseasonable hour?

SYLVIA: That's a secret you will be obliged to keep for your own sake. I see lights in the great hall. Whatever is the matter? Sir Davy and all the family are up.

COURTINE: They'll catch me here. Well, now you have brought me into this condition, what will you do with me, ha?

SYLVIA: You won't be contented for a while to be tied like a jade to an empty rack without hay, will you?

COURTINE: Faith, take me and put thy brand upon me quickly that if I light into strange hands they may know me for a sheep of thine.

SYLVIA: If it must be so, come, follow your shepherdess. Ba-a-a.

SCENE TWO

Another room in SIR DAVY's house.

Enter SIR DAVY and VERMIN.

SIR DAVY: I shall never sleep again. I have prayed so long were I to be hanged presently I have never a prayer left to help myself. I was no sooner lain down upon the bed and fallen into a slumber but methought the devil was carrying me down Ludgate Hill a-gallop, six puny fiends with flaming fire-forks running before him to throw me headlong into Fleet ditch which seemed to be turned into a lake of fire and brimstone. Would it were morning!

VERMIN: Truly, sir, it has been a very dismal night.

SIR DAVY: But didst thou meet a white thing upon the stairs?

VERMIN: No, sir, not I but methought I saw our great dog Towser with his brass collar on stand at the cellar-door as I came along the old entry.

SIR DAVY: It could never be. Towser has a chain. Had this thing a chain on?

VERMIN: No, sir, no chain but it had Towser's eyes for all the world.

SIR DAVY: What, ugly, great, frightful eyes?

VERMIN: Ay, huge saucer eyes but mightily like Towser's.

SIR DAVY: O Lord! O Lord! Hark! Hark!

VERMIN: What? What, I beseech you, sir!

SIR DAVY: What's that upon the stairs? Didst thou hear nothing? Hist, hark! Pat, pat, pat. Hark, hey!

VERMIN: Hear nothing? Where, sir?

SIR DAVY: Look! Look! What's that? What's that? In the corner there?

VERMIN: Where?

SIR DAVY: There.

VERMIN: What, upon the iron chest?

SIR DAVY: No, the long black thing up by the old clock-case. See! See! Now it stirs and is coming this way.

VERMIN: Alas, sir, speak to it. You are a Justice o' th' Peace. I beseech you. I dare not stay in the house. I'll call the watch and tell 'em Hell's broke loose. What shall I do? O!

Exit VERMIN.

SIR DAVY: O Vermin, if thou art a true servant have pity on thy master and do not forsake me in this distressed condition. Satan, be gone! I defy thee! I'll repent and be saved. I'll say my prayers. I'll go to church. Help! Help! Help! Was there anything or no? In what hole shall I hide myself?

Exit SIR DAVY.

Enter SIR JOLLY JUMBLE and FOURBIN.

SIR JOLLY: That should be Sir Davy's voice. The waiting-woman told me he was afraid and could not sleep. Pretty fellow, you've done your business handsomely. I'll warrant you have been a-whoring now, ha! You do well, I like you the better for't. What's o'clock?

FOURBIN: Near four, sir. 'Twill not be day yet these two hours.

SIR JOLLY: You have a sharp nose and are a nimble fellow. I have no more to say to you. Stand aside and be ready when I call. Here he comes. Hist! Hem, hem, hem.

Enter SIR DAVY.

SIR DAVY: Ha! What art thou?
Approach thou like the rugged Bankside bear,
The Eastcheap bull or monster shown in fair.
Take any shape but that and I'll confront thee.

SIR JOLLY: Alas, unhappy man! I am thy friend.

SIR DAVY: Thou canst not be my friend for I defy thee. Sir Jolly! Neighbour! Ha! Is it you? Are you sure it is you? Are you? Yourself? If you be, give me your hand. Alas-a-day, I ha' seen the devil.

SIR JOLLY: The devil, neighbour!

SIR DAVY: Ay, ay, there's no help for't. At first I fancied it was a young white bear's cub dancing in the shadow of my candle. Then it was turned to a pair of blue breeches with wooden legs on, stamped about the room as if all the cripples in town had kept their rendezvous there, when all of a sudden it appeared like a leather serpent and with a dreadful clap of thunder flew out the window.

SIR JOLLY: Thunder? Why, I heard no thunder.

SIR DAVY: What, were you asleep?

SIR JOLLY: 'Asleep'? No, no, no sleeping this night for me, I assure you.

SIR DAVY: Well, what's the best news then? How does the man?

SIR JOLLY: E'en as he did before he was born. Nothing at all. He's dead.

SIR DAVY: Dead! What, quite dead?

SIR JOLLY: As good as dead, if not quite dead. 'Twas a horrid murder – and then the terror of conscience, neighbour.

SIR DAVY: And, truly, I have a very terrified one, friend, though I never found I had any conscience at all till now. Pray, whereabout was his death's wound?

SIR JOLLY: Just here, just under his left pap – a dreadful gash.

SIR DAVY: So very wide?

SIR JOLLY: O, as wide as my hat. You might have seen his lungs, liver and heart as perfectly as if you had been in his belly.

SIR DAVY: Is there no way to have him privately buried and conceal this murder? Must I needs be hanged by the neck like a dog, neighbour? Do I look as if I would be hanged?

SIR JOLLY: Truly, Sir Davy, I must deal faithfully with you. You do look a little suspiciously at present. But have you seen the devil, say you?

SIR DAVY: Ay, surely, it was the devil. Nothing else could have frighted me so.

SIR JOLLY: Bless us and guard us all the angels! What's that?

SIR DAVY DUNCE kneels, holding up his hands and muttering as if he prayed.

SIR DAVY: Potestati sempiternae cuius benevolentia servantur gentes, et cuius misericordia.

SIR JOLLY: Neighbour, where are you, friend, Sir Davy?

SIR DAVY: Ah, whatever you do, be sure to stand close to me. Where is it?

SIR JOLLY: Just there, in the shape of a coach and six horses against the wall.

SIR DAVY: Deliver us all. He won't carry me away in that coach and six, will he?

SIR JOLLY: Do you see it?

Exit SIR JOLLY JUMBLE.

SIR DAVY: See it! Plain, plain. Dear friend, advise me what I shall do? Sir Jolly, Sir Jolly, do you hear nothing? Sir Jolly! Ha! Has he left me alone? Vermin!

Enter VERMIN.

VERMIN: Sir.

SIR DAVY: Am I alive? Dost thou know me again? Am I thy master, Sir Davy Dunce?

VERMIN: I hope I shall never forget you, sir.

SIR DAVY: Didst thou see nothing?

VERMIN: Yes, sir, methought the house was all o' fire.

SIR DAVY: Didst thou not see how the devils grinned and gnashed their teeth at me, Vermin?

VERMIN: Alas, sir, I was afraid one of 'em would have bit off my nose as he vanished out of the door.

SIR DAVY: Lead me away. I'll go to my wife. I'll die by my own dear wife. Run away to the Temple and call my lawyer. I'll make over my estate. I shan't live till noon. I'll give all I have to my wife, ha, Vermin!

VERMIN: Truly, sir, she's a very good lady.

SIR DAVY: Ah much, much too good for me, Vermin. Thou canst not imagine what she has done for me, man. She would break her heart if I should give anything away from her, she loves me so dearly. Yet if I do die thou shalt have all my old shoes.

VERMIN: I hope to see you live many a fair day yet.

SIR DAVY: Ah my wife, my poor wife! Lead me to my poor wife.

SCENE THREE

LADY DUNCE's bedchamber.

Scene draws and discovers BEAUGARD and LADY DUNCE in her chamber, SIR JOLLY watching.

LADY DUNCE: What think you now of a cold, wet march over the mountains, your men tired, your baggage not come up, at night a dirty, watery plain to encamp upon and nothing to shelter you but an old leather cloak as tattered as your flag? Is not this much better now than lying wet and getting the sciatica?

BEAUGARD: The hope of this made all fatigue easy to me. The thoughts of Clarinda have a thousand times refreshed me in my solitude. Whene'er I marched I fancied it was to my Clarinda! When I fought I imagined it was for my Clarinda! But when I came home and found Clarinda lost! How could you think of wasting but a night in the rank arms of that foul-feeding monster, that rotten trunk of a man, that lays claim to you?

LADY DUNCE: The persuasion of friends and the authority of parents.

BEAUGARD: And had you no more grace than to be ruled by a father and mother?

LADY DUNCE: When you were gone who should have given me better counsel how I could help myself?

BEAUGARD: Methinks you might have found some cleanlier shift to have thrown yourself upon than nauseous old age and unwholesome deformity.

LADY DUNCE: What, upon some overgrown, full-fed country fool with a horse face, a great ugly head and a great fine estate? One that should have been drained and squeezed and jolted up and down the town in hackneys with cheats and so sent home at three o'clock every morning like a lolling booby, stinking, with a belly full of stummed wine, and nothing in's pockets?

BEAUGARD: You might have made a tractable beast of such a one. He would have been young enough for training.

LADY DUNCE: Is youth then so gentle? Young men, like springs wrought by a subtle workman, easily ply to what their wishes press 'em but, the desire once gone that kept 'em down, they soon start straight again.

SIR JOLLY: (*At the door, peeping.*) So, so. Who says I see anything now? I see nothing, not I. I don't see, I don't see. I don't look, not so much as look, not I.

Enter SIR DAVY. SIR JOLLY JUMBLE comes forward.

SIR DAVY: I will have my wife. Carry me to my wife. I'll live and die with my wife, let the devil do his worst. Ah, my wife, my wife, my wife!

LADY DUNCE: (*Aside, to BEAUGARD.*) Alas, alas, we are ruined. Shift for yourself. Counterfeit the dead corpse once more or anything.

BEAUGARD feigns dead.

SIR DAVY: Ha! Whatsoe'er thou art, thou canst not eat me! Speak to me. Who has done this? Thou canst not say I did it.

SIR JOLLY: 'Did it'? Did what? Here's nobody says you did anything that I know, neighbour. What's the matter with you? What ails you? Whither do you go? Whither do you run? I tell you here's nobody says a word to you.

SIR DAVY: Did you not see the ghost just now?

SIR JOLLY: Ghost! Prithee now, here's no ghost. Whither would you go? I tell you, you shall not stir one foot farther, man. The devil take me if you do. Ghost! Prithee, here's no ghost at all. A little flesh and blood indeed there is – some old, some young, some alive, some dead and so forth. But ghost! Pish, here's no ghost.

SIR DAVY: But, sir, if I say I did see a ghost, I did see a ghost. (*To LADY DUNCE.*) Ah my dear, if thou hadst but seen the devil half so often as I have seen him.

LADY DUNCE: Alas, Sir Davy, if you ever loved me, come not, O come not near me. I have resolved to waste the short remainder of my life in penitence and taste of joys no more.

SIR DAVY: Alas, my poor child! (*To SIR JOLLY.*) But do you think then there was no ghost indeed?

SIR JOLLY: Ghost! Alas-a-day, what should a ghost do here?

SIR DAVY: And is the man dead?

SIR JOLLY: Dead? Ay, ay, stark dead. He's stiff by this time.

LADY DUNCE: Here you may see the horrid, ghastly spectacle, the sad effects of my too rigid virtue and your too fierce resentment.

SIR JOLLY: Do you see there?

SIR DAVY: Ay, ay, I do see. Would I had never seen him. Would he had lain with my wife in every house between Charing Cross and Aldgate so this had never happened.

SIR JOLLY: In troth and would he had. But we are all mortal, neighbour, all mortal. Today we are here, tomorrow gone like the shadow that vanisheth, like the grass that withereth or like the flower that fadeth or indeed like anything or rather like nothing. We are all mortal.

SIR DAVY: Heigh!

LADY DUNCE: (*Aside to BEAUGARD.*) Down, down that trap-door. It goes into a bathing-room. For the rest, leave it to me.

BEAUGARD descends through the trap-door, unseen by SIR DAVY.

SIR JOLLY: 'Tis very unfortunate that you should run yourself into this, Sir David.

SIR DAVY: Indeed it is.

SIR JOLLY: A man in authority, a person of years, one that used to go to church with his neighbours.

SIR DAVY: Every Sunday, truly, Sir Jolly. 'Tis very hard to ride in a cart and be hanged on a sunshiny morning to give butchers and apprentices a holiday. I'll run away.

SIR JOLLY: Run away? Why then your estate will be forfeited. You'll lose your estate, man.

SIR DAVY: Truly, you say right, friend, and a man had better be half-hanged than lose his estate, you know.

SIR JOLLY: Hanged? No, no, I think there's no great fear of hanging. What, the fellow was but a sort of an unaccountable fellow as I heard you say.

SIR DAVY: Ay, a pox on him. He was a soldierly sort of a vagabond. He had little or nothing but his sins to live upon. If I could have had but patience, he would have been hanged within these two months and all this mischief saved.

BEAUGARD rises up like a ghost at a trap-door, just before SIR DAVY.

Ah Lord! The devil, the devil, the devil!

SIR DAVY falls upon his face. BEAUGARD goes down the trap-door.

SIR JOLLY: Why, Sir Davy, Sir Davy, what ails you? What's the matter with you?

SIR DAVY: Let me alone, let me lie still. I will not look up to see an angel. Oh-h-h!

LADY DUNCE: My dear, why do you do these cruel things to affright me? Pray rise and speak to me.

SIR DAVY: I dare not stir. I saw the ghost again now.

LADY DUNCE: 'Ghost again'? What ghost? Where?

SIR DAVY: Why, there, there.

SIR JOLLY: Here has been no ghost.

SIR DAVY: Why, did you see nothing then?

LADY DUNCE: See nothing! No, nothing but one another.

SIR DAVY: Then I am enchanted or my end near at hand. For heaven's sake, neighbour, advise me what I shall do to be at rest.

SIR JOLLY: Do! Why, what think you if the body were removed?

SIR DAVY: Removed! I'd give a hundred pound the body were out of my house. Maybe then the devil would not be so impudent.

SIR JOLLY: I have discovered a door-place in the wall betwixt my lady's chamber and one that belongs to me. If you think fit, we'll beat it down and remove this troublesome lump of earth to my house.

SIR DAVY: But will ye be so kind?

SIR JOLLY: If you think it may by any means be serviceable to you.

SIR DAVY: Truly, if the body were removed and disposed of privately that no more might be heard of the matter. (*Aside.*) I hope he'll be as good as his word.

SIR JOLLY: Fear nothing. But, in troth, I had forgot one thing, utterly forgot it.

SIR DAVY: What's that?

SIR JOLLY: Why, it will be absolutely necessary that my lady stay with me at my house for one day till things are better settled.

SIR DAVY: Ah Sir Jolly! Whatever you think fit, anything of mine you have a mind to. Pray take her, you shall be very welcome. Hear you, my dearest? There is but one way for us to get rid of this untoward business and Sir Jolly has found it out. Therefore by all means go along with him and be ruled by him and whatever Sir Jolly would have thee do to it, heaven prosper ye. Good-bye, till I see you again.

Exit SIR DAVY.

SIR JOLLY: This is certainly the civillest cuckold in city, town or country.

BEAUGARD steps out of the trap-door.

BEAUGARD: Is he gone?

LADY DUNCE: Yes and has left poor me here.

BEAUGARD: In troth, madam, 'tis barbarously done, to commit a horrid murder on the body of an innocent poor fellow and then leave you to stem the danger of it.

SIR JOLLY: Od, were I as thee, sweetheart, I'd be revenged on him for it. Go, get ye together. Steal out of the house as softly as you can. I'll meet ye in the Piazza. Go. Don't let Sir Davy see you. Fourbin!

Enter FOURBIN.

FOURBIN: I am here, sir.

SIR JOLLY: Go you to my house. Tell my maids I am home in a trice. Bid 'em get the great chamber and a banquet ready and – d'ye hear? – carry the minstrels with ye too for I'm resolved to rejoice this morning.

Exit FOURBIN.

Let me see –

Enter SIR DAVY.

Sir Davy?

SIR DAVY: Is the business done? I cannot be satisfied till I am sure. Have you removed the body?

SIR JOLLY: Yes, yes, my servants conveyed it out of the house. Well, Sir Davy, a good morning to you. I wish you your health with all my heart, Sir Davy.

SIR DAVY: God-b'-w'-y' heartily, good neighbour.

Exit SIR JOLLY.

Vermin!

Enter VERMIN.

VERMIN: Did your honour call?

SIR DAVY: Go, run, run over the square and call the constable. Tell him here's murder committed and I must speak with him instantly.

Exit VERMIN.

I'll lead him to my neighbour's that he may find the dead body there and so let my neighbour be very fairly hanged in my stead. Ha! A very good jest as I hope to live. Ha, ha, ha! Hey, what's that?

WATCHMEN: (*At the door.*) Almost four o'clock and a dark, cloudy morning. Good-morrow, my masters all, good-morrow.

Enter CONSTABLE and WATCHMEN.

CONSTABLE: How's this! A door open! Come in, gentlemen. Ah, Sir Davy! Your honour's humble servant! I and my watch going my morning rounds and finding your door wide open made bold to enter to see there were no danger.

SIR DAVY: O Mr Constable, I'm glad you're here. I sent my man just now to call you. I have sad news to tell you, Mr Constable.

CONSTABLE: I am sorry for that, sir. Sad news?

SIR DAVY: O ay, very sad news truly. Here has been murder committed.

CONSTABLE: Murder! If that's all, we are your humble servants, sir. We'll bid you good-morrow. Murder's nothing at this time o' night in Covent Garden.

SIR DAVY: O, but this is a horrid, bloody murder done under my nose. I cannot but take notice of it though I am sorry to tell you the authors of it, very sorry truly.

CONSTABLE: Was it committed near at hand?

SIR DAVY: Oh, at the very next door. A sad murder indeed. After they had done, they carried the body into my neighbour Jolly's house. I am sorry to tell you, Mr Constable, for I am afraid it will look scurvily on his side but I am a Justice o' th' Peace, gentlemen, and am bound by my oath.

FIRST WATCHMAN: I never liked that Sir Jolly.

CONSTABLE: He threatened me t'other day for carrying a little, dirty, draggle-tailed whore to Bridewell and said she was his cousin. Sir, we'll go search his house.

SIR DAVY: Oh by all means, gentlemen. Justice must have its course. The king's subjects must not be destroyed. Vermin, carry Mr Constable and his dragons into the cellar and make 'em drink. I'll step into my study, put on my face of authority and call upon ye instantly.

ALL WATCHMEN: We thank your honour.

SCENE FOUR

SIR JOLLY JUMBLE's house

A banquet. Enter SIR JOLLY JUMBLE, BEAUGARD and LADY DUNCE and MUSICIANS.

SIR JOLLY: So, are ye come? I am glad of't. Od, you're welcome, very welcome, od, ye are. Here's a small banquet but I hope 'twill please you. Sit ye down, sit ye down, both together – nay, both together. A pox o' him that parts ye, I say.

BEAUGARD: Sir Jolly, this might be an entertainment for Antony and Cleopatra were they living.

SIR JOLLY: Pish! A pox on Antony and Cleopatra! They are dead and rotten long ago. Come, come, time's short, time's short and must be made the best use of – for

(*Sings.*) Youth's a flower that soon does fade,
And life is but a span
Man was for woman made
And woman made for man.

Why, now we can be bold and make merry and frisk and be brisk, rejoice and make a noise and – od, I am pleased, mightily pleased, od, I am.

LADY DUNCE: Really, Sir Jolly, you are more a philosopher than I thought you were.

SIR JOLLY: Philosopher, madam? Yes, madam, I have read books in my times. Od, Aristotle, in some things, had very pretty notions, he was an understanding fellow. Why don't ye eat? Here, child, here's some ringoes. Help your neighbour a little. Od, they are very good, very comfortable, very cordial.

BEAUGARD: Sir Jolly, your health.

SIR JOLLY: With all my heart, old boy.

LADY DUNCE: Dear Sir Jolly, what are these? I never tasted these before.

SIR JOLLY: That! Eat it, eat it – eat it when I bid you. Od, 'tis the root satyrion, a very precious plant. I gather 'em every May myself. Od, they'll make an old fellow of sixty-five cut a caper like a dancing-master. Give me some wine. Madam, here's a health, here's a health, madam. Here's a health to honest Sir Davy, faith and troth. Ha, ha, ha!

Dance.

Enter FOURBIN.

FOURBIN: Sir, sir, sir! What will you do? The constable and all his watch are at the door and threaten demolishment if not admitted.

SIR JOLLY: Od's so! The constable and his watch! What's to be done now? Get ye both into the alcove there. Get ye gone quickly, quickly. No noise, no noise, d'ye hear? A pox on the constable and his watch! What the devil have they to do here?

Scene shuts upon LADY DUNCE and BEAUGARD.

Enter CONSTABLE, WATCHMEN and SIR DAVY. SIR JOLLY comes forward.

CONSTABLE: This way, gentlemen. Stay one of ye at the door and let nobody pass, do you hear? Sir Jolly, your servant.

SIR JOLLY: What! This outrage, this disturbance committed upon my house! Sir, sir, sir! What do you mean by these doings, sweet sir? Ho!

CONSTABLE: Sir, having received information that the body of a murdered man is concealed in your house, I am come, according to my duty, to make search and discover the truth. (*To the* WATCHMEN.) Stand to my assistance, gentlemen.

SIR JOLLY: A murdered man, sir?

SIR DAVY: Yes, a murdered man, sir. Sir Jolly, I am sorry to see a person of your figure in the parish concerned in murder, I say.

SIR JOLLY: Here's a dog! Here's a rogue for you! Here's a villain! Here's a cuckoldly son of his mother! I never knew a cuckold in my life that was not a false rogue in his heart. There are no honest fellows living but whoremasters. Hark you, sir, what a pox do you mean?

SIR DAVY: When your worship's come to be hanged you'll find the meaning of't, sir. I say once more, search the house.

CONSTABLE: It shall be done, sir. Come along, friends.

Exeunt CONSTABLE *and* WATCHMEN *with* SIR DAVY.

SIR JOLLY: Search my house! O Lord, what will become of me? I shall lose my reputation with man and woman and nobody will ever trust me again! All will be discovered, do what I can. I'll sing a song like a dying swan and try to give 'em warning.

(*Sings.*) Go from the window, my love, my love, my love,
Go from the window, my dear.
The wind and the rain
Has brought 'em back again
And thou canst have no lodging here.
O Lord, search my house!

SIR DAVY: (*Offstage.*) Break down that door. I'll have that door broke open. Break down that door, I say.

Knocking within.

SIR JOLLY: Very well done! Break down my doors! Break down my walls, gentlemen! Plunder my house! Ravish my maids! Ah, cursed be cuckolds, cuckolds, constables and cuckolds!

Scene draws and discovers BEAUGARD and LADY DUNCE. Enter SIR DAVY, CONSTABLE and WATCHMEN.

BEAUGARD: (*Drawing his sword.*) Stand off! By heaven, the first that comes here comes upon his death.

SIR DAVY: Sir, your humble servant. I am glad to see you are alive again with all my heart. (*To the CONSTABLE and WATCHMEN.*) Gentlemen, here's no harm done, gentlemen. Here's nobody murdered, gentlemen. The man's alive again, gentlemen. But here's my wife, gentlemen, and a fine gentleman with her, gentlemen and Mr Constable. I hope you'll bear me witness, Mr Constable.

BEAUGARD: Hark ye, ye curs. Keep off from snapping at my heels or I shall so feague ye.

SIR JOLLY: Get ye gone, ye dogs, ye rogues, ye night-toads of the parish dungeon. Disturb my house at these unseasonable hours! Get ye out of my doors or I'll brain ye. Dogs, rogues, villains!

Exeunt CONSTABLE and WATCHMEN.

BEAUGARD: And next, for you, Sir Coxcomb. You see I am not murdered though you paid well for the performance. What think you of bribing my own man to butcher me?

Enter FOURBIN and BLOODY BONES.

Look ye, sir, he can cut a throat upon occasion and here's another dresses a man's heart with oil and pepper better than any cook in Christendom.

FOURBIN: Will your worship please to have one for your breakfast this morning?

SIR DAVY: With all my heart, sweetheart. Anything in the world, faith and troth. (*Aside.*) Ha, ha, ha! This is the purest sport. Ha, ha, ha!

Enter VERMIN.

VERMIN: Oh, sir, the most unhappy and most unfortunate news! There has been a gentleman in madam Sylvia's chamber all this night who, just as you went out of doors, carried her away. Whither they are gone nobody knows.

SIR DAVY: With all my heart, I am glad of't, child. I would not care if he had carried away my house and all, man. (*Aside.*) 'Unhappy news'! Poor fool, he does not know I am a cuckold and that anybody may make bold with what belongs to me. Ha, ha, ha! I think I was never so pleased in all my life. Ha, ha, ha!

Enter SYLVIA, followed by COURTINE.

SYLVIA: Sir Jolly, ah Sir Jolly, protect me or I'm ruined.

SIR JOLLY: My little minikin, is it thy squeak?

BEAUGARD: My dear Courtine, welcome.

SIR JOLLY: Well, child, child, and what would that wicked fellow do to thee?

SYLVIA: O, sir, he has most inhumanly seduced me out of my uncle's house and threatens to marry me.

SIR JOLLY: In troth, that's very uncivilly done. I don't like these marriages. I'll have no marriages in my house and there's an end of't.

BEAUGARD: And do you intend to marry his niece, Ned?

COURTINE: Yes, and never ask his consent neither.

SIR DAVY: In troth, that's very well said. I am glad with all my heart, man, because she has five thousand pound to her portion and my estate's bound to pay it. Well, this is the happiest day. Ha, ha, ha!

Here, take thy bride, like man and wife agree
And may she prove as true as mine to me.

BEAUGARD: Ned, I wish thee joy. Thou art come opportunely to be a witness of a perfect reconcilement between that worthy knight Sir Davy Dunce and me which to preserve inviolate (*To SIR DAVY.*) you must, sir, before we part, enter into such covenants as I shall think fit.

SIR DAVY: No more to be said. It shall be done, sweetheart. But don't be too hard upon me. Use me gently, as thou didst my wife. Gently. Ha, ha, ha! A very good jest, i'faith! Ha, ha, ha!

BEAUGARD: Nay, sir, there are laws even for cut-throats. As you tender your future credit, take this wronged lady home and use her handsomely. Use her like my mistress, sir, do you mark me, that when we think fit to meet again I hear no complaint of you. This must be done, friend.

SIR JOLLY: In troth, it is but reasonable, very reasonable in troth.

LADY DUNCE: Can you, my dear, forgive me one misfortune?

SIR DAVY: Madam, in one word, I am thy ladyship's most humble servant, Sir Davy Dunce, knight, living in Covent Garden.